THORNETT · KEN CATCHPOLE · SIM

SE · MICHAEL LYNAGH · ARR-

BURKE · GEORGE GR PHEN

ERS · TREVOR ALLAN · JOHN THOR

ARK ELLA · DAVID CAMPESE · MICH

AN · JOHN EALES · MATTHEW BURKE

GEORGE SMITH · CYRIL TOWERS · T

POLE · SIMON POIDEVIN · MARK ELL

RR-JONES · TIM HORAN · JOHN EAL

TEPHEN LARKHAM · GEORGE SMITH

NETT · KEN CATCHPOLE · SIMON PO

L LYNAGH · NICK FARR-JONES · TIM

GE GREGAN · STEPHEN LARKHAM · G

JOHN THORNETT · KEN CATCHPO

CAMPESE · MICHAEL LYNAGH · NICI

TTHEW BURKE · GEORGE GREGAN ·

ERS · TREVOR ALLAN · JOHN THOR

ARK ELLA · DAVID CAMPESE · MICH

AN · JOHN EALES · MATTHEW BURKE

GEORGE SMITH · CYRIL TOWERS · T

POLE · SIMON POIDEVIN · MARK ELL

RR-JONES · TIM HORAN · JOHN EAL

The

IMMORTALS

of Australian Rugby Union

The

IMMORTALS

— *of* Australian Rugby Union —

Gordon Bray

GELDING STREET PRESS

A Gelding Street Press book
An imprint of Rockpool Publishing

PO Box 252
Summer Hill
NSW 2130 Australia

www.geldingstreetpress.com

ISBN: 9781922662033

Published in Australia in 2024 by Rockpool Publishing

Alamy: vi, viii, 3, 20, 40, 58, 60, 66, 74, 78, 84, 92, 94, 100, 132, 188, 194 • Newspix:
4, 24, 27, 28, 34, 37, 45, 46, 49, 56, 62, 65, 70, 74, 77, 88, 99, 103, 104, 106, 110,
113 (both), 114, 116, 118, 119, 120, 123, 124, 127, 130, 135, 136, 139, 142, 147,
148, 151, 152, 154, 159, 160, 163, 164, 166, 168, 171, 172, 175, 176, 192 • Towers
family collection: 6, 11, 14 • Waverley College: 15 • ABC Document Archives: 23,
69 • Portrait by John Williams (supplied by Patrick Badger) • Brett Dooley: 50, 59 •
Simon Poidevin archives: 52 • Rugby Australia archives: 8, 16, 33, 42, 55, 87 (both),
91 • Photographer unknown: 198 • Gordon Bray supplied: 81 • Campese family:
82 • Farr-Jones family: 96 (both) • Horan family archive: 108 (all) • Australia Post:
128 • Burke family: 140 • Nine Licensing/Fairfax Media: 144, 186 • Larkham
family: 156 • SANZAAR: 177 • Heidi Hemming (supplied by Patrick Badger):
178 • John White/Peter Johnson pic/portrait (supplied by Patrick Badger): 179

Design and typesetting by Christine Armstrong, Rockpool Publishing
Acquisition editor: Luke West, Rockpool Publishing
Edited by Heather Millar

NATIONAL
LIBRARY
OF AUSTRALIA

A catalogue record for this
book is available from the
National Library of Australia

Printed and bound in China

10 9 8 7 6 5 4 3 2 1

DEDICATION

For my wife Catherine and children Anna and
Andrew, who have diligently shared my rugby
journey. Their love and passionate support have
always been an inspiration and a source of sheer joy.
They are the pulse of my life.

Australia captain John Thornett is chaired off by teammate Phil Hawthorne (right) and rival Barbarians captain Noel Murphy after the Wallabies' victory at Cardiff Arms Park in 1967.

CONTENTS

David Campese captivated the rugby world with his attacking brilliance.

INTRODUCTION

The Immortals of Australian Rugby Union is the ninth book in Rockpool Publishing/Gelding Street Press's 'Immortals of Australian Sport' series and the fifth devoted to a team sport. Given that the 11 cricketers, 11 soccer players and 13 rugby league players celebrated in previous editions corresponded with the number of players in their respective teams, the task of selecting 15 Wallaby 'Immortals' from the past 125 years offered a slight numerical advantage. Importantly, it also provided an opportunity to add further worthy recipients.

Rugby league, which was professional from the outset and evolved from rugby union, first developed the concept of anointing their foremost players as 'immortals'. League adheres to a policy of elevating very few of their leading figures to this rare honour and acknowledgement. As stated in *The Immortals of Australian Rugby League,* 'The immortals concept has become an established part of the Australian rugby league scene. It honours a very select group of former players regarded as the game's elite. These players weren't just high achievers and standout performers, but also influential identities who set a new benchmark and changed the way rugby league is played.'

As the author of *The Immortals of Australian Rugby Union* I endorse those selection criteria, and they have provided the guiding principles for the other volumes in the series. Rugby Australia's equivalent – the Wallabies Hall of Fame – is much broader and numerically less exclusive. It already includes more than 50 inductees since it was established in 2005. It is less restrictive, and specifically celebrates and recognises 'our Wallabies who made a major contribution to the game of Rugby both on and off the Rugby field.'

My challenge was to select 15 established legends regardless of their era – players who achieved fame on the global rugby stage through their deeds on the field and their impact and demeanour off it. These would be Wallabies who either earned individual World XV status or were a dominant influence in a world champion team or equivalent. Like the rugby league Immortals, they must be individuals who changed the way the game was played and left indelible memories for those lucky enough to have witnessed their exploits. My own observation of players stretches back 65 years to childhood in the late 1950s. As well, I have enjoyed a personal connection with some of the older nominated Immortals through my 50-plus years as a sports broadcaster.

The task of selection highlighted one of rugby's most endearing qualities: it is a game that embraces all shapes and sizes. Two of the Immortals in this book clearly demonstrate that factor. Ken Catchpole stood just 5 feet 5 inches (1.65 m) and weighed 10 stone (63.5 kg); John Eales was a towering 6 feet 7 inches (2.01 m) and 18 stone (115 kg). They starred in totally different eras but, significantly, both were world-beaters, genuine champions whose feats took your breath away. There is a place for everybody in rugby union. That is the essence of its greatness and universal appeal.

Test rugby began in Australia in 1899. Acknowledgment must be made of Herbert Henry 'Dally'

Messenger who was the standout Australian player of the pre-First World War era. His defection from rugby union to rugby league gave the new code a credibility that enabled it to weather the earlier crisis of a disastrous tour of the United Kingdom in 1908. Messenger was the David Campese of his generation – a brilliant, effective, confident and imaginative player in his ploys to defeat opponents and score tries. Messenger was a match-winner and darling of the crowds yet played only two Test matches.

The First Wallabies (not that they were initially known as such) to tour Britain, USA and Canada in 1908–09 were captained by Dr Herb Moran. They won 32 of their 38 matches including winning the Olympic gold medal for rugby. After their arrival in England a local newspaper raised the idea of a nickname for the team. 'Rabbits', 'Wallaroos' and 'Waratahs' were all suggested but after a player meeting 'Wallabies' emerged victorious by just a few votes. Winger Charles 'Boxer' Russell starred on that tour with 24 tries and was one of several players approached on tour by a NSW Rugby League official to switch codes. Russell and Messenger

Strength. Speed. Skill. Tim Horan was the full package and one of international rugby's greatest ever centres.

are just two of many legendary Wallaby players who failed to make my final Immortal list.

    Wallaby Greats is a loving account of 25 Wallabies compiled by a former Wallaby and academic Max Howell and his wife Lingyu Xie. They included Tom Lawton Snr in their honour roll. Again, he is an example of a player who met the criteria but didn't squeeze into my top XV. Max's essay details what a brilliant all-round schoolboy athlete (and scholar) Lawton was. He played rugby league at university after service in France as a gunner

because it was the only rugby code available in Queensland at the time. Lawton was an integral member of the wonderful Waratahs side that toured Britain and France in 1927–28 and helped develop the 'Waratah' game – an intense and skilful system based on the notion that the ball should never be kicked unless in the direst circumstances. Lawton captained the Wallabies to their 3-0 series win over the All Blacks in 1929 and returned to Queensland to revive rugby union in Brisbane. He was undoubtedly a world class player and influential identity who helped change the way the game was played. Lawton's exploits demonstrate the daunting challenge of selecting 15 Wallaby Immortals from a cohort of over 900. As Howell explained, 'Every Wallaby by a matter of selection is a great, but we all acknowledge there are super-greats, whose performances exceed that of the other greats.'

Comparing all-time greats from different eras is a very subjective and contentious exercise. Rugby was an amateur sport in Australia until the beginning of the 1996 season when the code went professional in response to a massive international TV rights deal. In the 1960s Wallabies were given one shilling a day while on major tours and, with few exceptions, were not paid by

Simon Poidevin is one of only four Australians – along with David Campese, Michael Lynagh and Nick Farr-Jones – to have won rugby union's Grand Slam, achieved a series victory in New Zealand, and won a Rugby World Cup.

their employers while playing away. At home they were 'part-timers' – amateurs who trained two nights a week and went to work during the day. Compare that scenario to the elite professional rugby player of today who is financially secure and pampered on and off the field in the quest to reach peak potential. I hope this book might help balance the scales by outlining the disadvantages endured by the distant legends of yesteryear. It is surely appropriate to recognise their astonishing efforts. To emphasise that point, I name my All-time Wallaby team including an eight-man bench. Coincidentally more than half the players made their Test debut at least 50 years ago. No doubt these will provoke much debate but that is the nature of the beast, and to employ an old cliché, rugby is always the winner.

The guiding brief of *The Immortals of Australian Rugby Union* was to explore the careers of the 15 chosen players and to provide a detailed overview of their accomplishments and what set them apart from other Immortal contenders. Each made a special and enduring impact on Australian Rugby. As a commentator I especially loved calling the great 'X factor' players – the ones who separated themselves from the rest by their individual on-field deeds yet still contributed within a team context. David Campese's surreal pass to Tim Horan at the 1991 World Cup; George Gregan's astonishing tackle on Jeff Wilson to save the Bledisloe Cup in 1994; John Eales' miracle penalty goal against the All Blacks in Wellington six years later. These were all instances of a master craftsman – a true Immortal – at work.

For all those legends who missed Immortal status in my selection there is a chapter of Honourable Mentions. Even that list does not include amazing Wallaby heroes like fullbacks Roger Gould, Alec Ross and Jim Lenehan; champion No. 8s Toutai Kefu and Tim Gavin; legendary front-rowers Ewen McKenzie, Stephen Moore and Tony 'Slaggy' Miller;; and mercurial flankers David Wilson, Col 'Breeze' Windon, David Pocock, Michael Hooper and Phil Waugh. In that sense my selection task was both joyous and at other times gut-wrenching. Welcome to my rugby world. In the famous words of Wallaby legend and my former co-commentator Chris Handy, 'Go you good things!'

Gordon Bray

Towers represented NSW a record 40 times and held the try scoring record for 14 years. He coached Randwick teams at all levels for over 50 years.

CYRIL TOWERS

Birthdate	30 July 1907 (died 8 June 1985)
Place of birth	Mansfield, Victoria
Nickname	Holden
Caps	19 (Wallaby #230)

Hailed as 'the thinking man's centre', Towers was a key figure in Wallaby sides for a decade from his debut, aged 19, in 1926. He burst onto the global rugby stage in 1927–28, starring on the famous Waratahs tour of the northern hemisphere. He was arguably Australia's greatest player of the pre-Second World War era. Despite being central to the team's many breakthrough successes against the All Blacks, he became a victim of rugby politics when controversially omitted from the 1933 Wallaby tour of South Africa, and the ill-fated 1939 British tour.

Cyril Towers' personality expressed his strength of character and fiercely independent nature. He was his own man – one who never shirked any challenge to his often passionate and well-reasoned views on rugby, and life in general. That mental toughness and resilience were developed at a vulnerable early age when his father, Tom, decided to abandon his young family in Melbourne and leave for a new life in Perth. The impact was devastating.

It is significant to acknowledge an early reference point for this future prophet and exponent of running rugby. Given his formative upbringing in Victoria, Cyril's exposure to Australian Rules football was inevitable. Playing that code helped craft his understanding of tactical kicking skills and the nuances of an oval ball. This undoubtedly aided the development

NEW SOUTH WALES RUGBY UNION TEAM.

"THE WARATAHS"

TOUR OF GREAT BRITAIN AND FRANCE, 1927-28.

	K. TARLETON	S. C. KING	E. E. FORD	G. C. GORDON	C. H. TOWERS	B. JUDD	J. B. EGAN	W. H. MANN	M. R. BLAIR
J. L. TANCRED	J. W. BRECKENRIDGE		G. BLAND	G. P. STOREY	J. FORD	A. N. FINLAY	E. N. GREATOREX	A. J. TANCRED	A. J. A. BOWERS
W. ROSS	Dr. W. J. B. SHEEHAN	T. LAWTON	A. C. WALLACE (Capt.)	E. GORDON SHAW (Manager)	C. L. FOX (Vice-Capt.)	E. J. THORN	J. G. BLACKWOOD	H. F. W
			J. L. DUNCAN		F. W. MEAGHER		S. MALCOLM	

(Official Photograph by J. E. THOMAS, 231 Chepstow Road, New

He was a member of the Waratahs' 1927-28 tour of Great Britain, France and North America. He is seen in the centre of the back row.

of his remarkably all-encompassing rugby skillset.

When his mother remarried, the family moved to Roma in Queensland before eventually deciding to settle permanently in Sydney. Fate then played its hand. Entry to high school brought exposure to rugby union thanks to two outstanding schoolboy coaches. At Randwick Boys' Intermediate High he was mentored by Oates Taylor who saw rugby as an ensemble game predominantly driven by running and passing, with limited kicking. A transfer to Waverley College then placed Towers under the tutelage of Arthur Hennessy. Cyril was captivated by the rugby intelligence of Oates and Hennessy and their attacking instincts shaped his philosophy. Through the Waverley connection Towers met future Waratah teammate Wally Meagher who, along with another future Wallaby, Len Palfreyman, introduced him to the Randwick District RUFC. It was the beginning of a lifelong love affair with the 'Galloping Greens' during which he set a club record of 233 first grade games.

Cyril's physical frame was blessed with lightning speed and an outside body swerve and change of pace that could beat the best defender. He possessed 'soft' hands and was a technically complete tackler. His analytical tactical prowess also set him apart. His grandson, Pat Howard, himself a 20-cap Wallaby and former European Player and Coach of the Year, remembers those insights. 'Whenever we sat down at the meal table Cyril would demonstrate strategies with salt and pepper shakers and kitchen utensils. It was a standard ritual and the whole family was a captive audience. His fertile rugby brain was astonishing and in a constant state of regeneration.'

In 1926 Towers made his 'Test' debut for NSW as a teenager against New Zealand alongside club-mate and scrum-half Meagher who was three years his senior. That match was one of 10 caps awarded posthumously to Cyril. (Because there was no national team between 1920 and 1928 the Australian Rugby Union eventually granted Test status to all Waratah matches against other nations played during that period.)

Meagher developed Randwick's traditional running game that championed a run/pass/support approach, with flatter alignment. His influences were Waverley College coach Hennessy and acclaimed

Waratahs' captain A.C. 'Johnnie' Wallace. Towers was an ardent disciple and associate of those three rugby luminaries and his growing reputation as an attacking centre with uncompromising defence quickly gained traction. He was selected for the nine-month 1927–28 Waratah tour of Great Britain and France which still enjoys treasured status in Australia's rugby heritage.

The celebrated Wallaby forward Peter 'Charlie' Crittle described that squad as 'the most significant team that ever left Australian shores'. In *For the Sake of the Game* by Peter Fenton, Crittle pinpointed the then revolutionary strategy of captain/coach Johnnie Wallace: 'He was of the firm belief that the Waratahs' best chance of success lay in exploiting the running and handling skills of all members of the team. Whenever possible, defence was to be turned into attack.'

By tour's end the Waratahs had played 31 matches for 24 wins, two draws and five losses. They won three Internationals against Wales, Ireland and France but lost to England and Scotland. The 21-year-old Towers missed the games against Wales and Scotland but was at outside-centre in the wins over Ireland and France and scored two tries in the 18-11 loss to England. Overall, he played 25 matches and was the leading try scorer with winger Eric Ford on 15. It was an impressive tour and the UK *Daily Express* reported: 'The Waratahs will not weep over a defeat or two. They played the game in the same spirit for over six months, and when the tour was over they left an indelible memory of 15-man rugby not seen before in the United Kingdom.'

Just months after returning home, the majority of the 29-strong tour party elected to stand down for the upcoming Test campaign in New Zealand. Towers was one of only three players who decided to back up. The average age of that Waratahs squad was just 22, making them the youngest team to visit New Zealand. Cyril played all 10 games and was the top point scorer and consistently the tourists' most influential player.

Although the main All Blacks team was on tour in South Africa, the Internationals were later given Test status by the Australian Rugby Union in a tightly contested series. The Waratahs played attacking rugby but could only manage one win, in the Third Test in Christchurch. Their poor goal-kicking had proved costly. The Aussies scored 10 tries

Towers was a beautifully balanced runner with explosive pace off the mark and distinctive body swerve.

Towers was the consummate defender, able to shut down attacking raids with ease.

to 5 but could only complete two conversions. Despite this, every game was close: the biggest winning margin in the whole series was three points. According to one local sportswriter: 'No visiting team had played more delightful rugby than these young Waratahs. Possessing extremely fast backs, the New South Welshmen threw the ball about in dazzling fashion and moved at such pace that they were dangerous even when in their own 25.'

Representative rugby returned to Queensland in 1928 after a 14-year hiatus. The national team was reinstated the following year and the stage was ready for a three-

Test home series against the NZ All Blacks. In July 1929 the great Queensland fly-half Tom Lawton was selected to lead the Wallabies in their historic return to Test rugby. The players wore green jumpers and a near capacity crowd of 40,000 witnessed a famous victory. Australia prevailed 9-8 after NZ flyer Alf Waterman lost the ball over the goal line near full-time. Towers had suffered an eye injury in the second half and missed the return clash at the Exhibition Ground in Brisbane. Australia won that game by 17-9 to clinch the series.

The exciting prospect now loomed of a historic 3-0 whitewash in Sydney. Recalled to join his established centre partner, Syd King, Cyril was instrumental in Australia's remarkable victory after New Zealand had cleared out to a 13-0 lead. He drop-kicked a penalty goal and had a strong hand in both Australian tries – scored by King and the outstanding No. 8, Jack Ford.

It was an epic milestone achieved. The All Blacks had never lost a three-Test series, let alone all three games. The Wallabies were back with a bang on the world stage. The Australian front row of 'Wild Bill' Cerutti and Queenslanders Eddie Bonis and Eddie Thompson were the unsung heroes of the series.

Australia franked their form the following year beating Great Britain 6-5 at the Sydney Cricket Ground (SCG) in front of 31,000 fans. Cyril delivered the final pass for both Wallaby tries. He also pulled off one of the great try saving tackles. Lions' flanker Ivor Jones was given an unobstructed run to the line after a perfect pass from centre Tony Novis who'd drawn fullback Alec Ross. But Towers then appeared from nowhere to torpedo Jones into touch with full-time beckoning.

Such was the force of Cyril's lunge that he crashed into the picket fence of the cricket ground and suffered a head injury that kept him off work for two months.

In 1933 Towers was a shock omission from the Wallaby touring party for South Africa. He'd missed most of the previous season due to injury but no-one had expected the selectors would make this controversial call. His class and experience were missed, and Australia lost the series 3-1. In *Australian Rugby*, celebrated sports journalist and author Jack Pollard gave this version of how the shock omission had come about: 'Team manager [coach] Dr Wally Matthews said Towers' forthrightness was so disruptive it would upset team morale and, forced to choose between Matthews and Towers, Towers was omitted.'

Down but not out, Cyril had the last laugh the following year against traditional rivals New Zealand. Skippered by dashing fullback Alec Ross, Australia won back the newly

'The All Blacks had never lost a three-Test series, let alone all three games. The Wallabies were back with a bang on the world stage.'

created Bledisloe Cup crunching the Kiwis 25-11 in the First Test, a record Wallaby margin against the All Blacks. Towers celebrated his return with two slashing tries. (The Second Test was drawn 3-3.)

But with the world still recovering from the Great Depression, Cyril had grown restless and he opted to bypass the 1936 tour of New Zealand. He had a burning ambition to live and play in South Africa, and to base himself at Port Elizabeth. But first, there was a more pressing goal – to attend the Berlin Olympics. After arriving in Genoa by ship he cycled to Hamburg to reunite with his surrogate father, uncle Tom Doyle, whose family had provided wonderful support to the Towers' clan during their early struggles.

Then, ever the fitness fanatic, Cyril decided to visit the US Track & Field team's training camp in Hamburg and soon found himself practising starts with the great American sprinter, Jesse Owens. Although Towers could beat Owens out of the starting blocks he was naturally soon hauled in by the disciplined athleticism of Owens. Nevertheless, the American legend was impressed by the initial explosive speed of

this rugby upstart from Down Under and the pair formed a warm relationship. (Owens went on to dominate the Berlin Games, winning the 100 m/200 m sprint double – setting a world record of 20.3 seconds in the 200 m – the long jump and 4 x 100 m relay.)

Rejuvenated by his stimulating adventure in Europe and South Africa, Towers was summoned back to Australia by his great mentor and former Waratah skipper, Johnnie Wallace, now the new Wallabies' coach. In 1937 Towers led NSW to a stunning 17-6 victory over the touring Springboks. The formidable visitors had no answer to the superb running and support skills of the Waratah backs who appreciated the firm conditions.

Now 30, Cyril was invited to captain his country for the first time at Test level. It was not an easy debut. The weather gods were unkind for the first of two Test matches at the SCG. A muddy, rain-sodden pitch nullified the attacking threat of the home side backs. In the first clash Towers converted his own try in the 9-5 loss. South Africa kept the ball close to their forwards and dominated possession, aided by the superb tactical kicking of Danie Craven who peppered touch resulting in a staggering 119 lineouts.

A week later in the Second Test, the Wallabies made seven changes, several forced by injury. The Boks ran up a staggering 26-6 half-time lead. Cyril left the field injured as Australia responded bravely with three unanswered tries. Flanker Keith Windon moved to centre and was instrumental in the comeback but South Africa held on to win 26-17. Hailed as the greatest ever Springbok team, those impressive tourists then crossed the Tasman to win their first Test series in New Zealand.

Sadly, Towers' distinguished playing career ended soon after with a shattering thud. In the final trial for the 1939 tour of Britain he was asked to captain 'The Rest' against the Australian team. The Rest won 48-3 and their skipper was best on field scoring two tries and setting up five others. What more could he do? But, alas, his name was missing when the team was read out by his nemesis, newly reinstated coach Dr Wally Matthews, then the Mayor of Orange. Matthews said Cyril was simply 'too strong a personality'.

Disenchanted with the game he had served so splendidly, Cyril announced his retirement the

Towers was a product of Waverley College in Sydney and the school's old boys' rugby club still marks his achievements on its website.

AUSTRALIA v NEW ZEALAND
SYDNEY CRICKET GROUND
1st TEST
11th AUGUST 1934
AUST. 26 defeated N.Z. 11

LEFT TO RIGHT
E DUNLOP (Vic) W G WHITE(Q) D BRIDLE(Vic) W MACKNEY (NSW) A HODGSON(NSW) C H TOWERS(NSW) D McLEAN(Q) V BIRMINGHAM(Q) E BONIS(Q) J D KELAHER(NSW) E S HAYES(Q) L LEWIS(Q) S J MALCOLM(NSW) E M JESSEP(Vice Capt Vic) A ROSS(Capt NSW)

The Australia team photo for the Test against New Zealand on 11 August 1934 shows Towers sixth from the left.

following year telling the *Daily Telegraph* he was fed up with the 'petty meddling and stupid administration. They've killed my enthusiasm for the game.' It was not an unfamiliar complaint. In *The Visitors* authors Chester and McMillan paid a fitting tribute: 'Cyril Towers returned from the Waratah [1927–28] tour as one of the stars of the team. In his prime he was hailed by many critics as the best centre in world rugby and was certainly one of the great Australian players of all time.'

Cyril continued to play for Randwick and he and Wally Meagher coached the club into the 1950s and often beyond on a part-time basis. It was a labour of love. After all, the pair had mortgaged their houses to help the 'Galloping Greens' acquire the new clubhouse. Cyril hadn't told his wife of that risky decision but the arrangement included a proviso that Meagher would manage the new club as they could not afford a misstep given their personal finances were on the line. The spirit of rugby ran strongly through the Towers family. He and wife Rita had two daughters and a son. One daughter Margariete married Wallaby prop John Howard and coached the Teachers/Norths 1st grade team. Lyn married Roy Prosser, another celebrated Wallaby prop. Grandson Pat Howard became a third-generation Wallaby. As Cyril joked to his daughters about signing on with two front-rowers: 'What were you girls thinking marrying props? You've both married the crust of the loaf of unsliced bread.'

Towers always maintained an extraordinary level of fitness and adherence to routine. He maintained his connection with elite rugby by joining the ABC-TV commentary team for the Saturday afternoon match telecasts. After completing his commentary duties he loved to then review the 'match of the day' over a few beers. You could usually find him with Norman May and other Sydney-based broadcasters at a favourite ABC 'watering hole', the Gladstone Hotel in Darlinghurst. But always at the prescribed time, with disseminations completed, he would announce his departure and promptly embark on the 90-minute trek from William Street to his

home in Maroubra – and he always set a cracking pace.

Towers remains a true giant of Australian rugby history. Lifelong mate Wally Meagher summed up Cyril's qualities in *Rugby News*: 'No fairer player has graced the field, and I cannot remember having seen an unsportsmanlike action by Cyril. No player in the game derives more enjoyment, evinces more keenness or at all times gives of his very best. His record of achievement and gentlemanly bearing have stamped him an everlasting ornament to the code and a football genius whose name will endure while ever Rugby Union is played.'

Trevor Allan was ever ready to open up an attack with one of his straight dashes upfield.

TREVOR ALLAN

Birthdate:	**27 September 1926 (died 27 January 2007)**
Place of birth:	**Bathurst, New South Wales**
Nickname:	**Tubby**
Caps:	**14 (Wallaby #323)**

'The boy centre' who became a man overnight, Allan established himself on the global rugby stage immediately after the Second World War. His lightning acceleration at outside-centre, silky handling and lethal defence defined his remarkable skills. In 1946, in just his first year out of school, he was selected for NSW after only six club games and three months later became a Wallaby. After regular skipper Bill McLean broke his leg during the successful 1947–48 Wallaby campaign in Britain, 'Tubby' Allan became Australia's youngest touring captain at 21 years of age. In 1949 he led the Wallabies to their first Bledisloe Cup series win on New Zealand soil.

Trevor Allan would not have been out of place in a *Boy's Own Annual*. Handsome, athletic and engagingly humble, he was embraced as a sporting hero at a time when the nation craved inspiration and positivity after enduring the pain and grief of the Second World War. Describing Allan's gifts in *Wallaby Greats*, author and teammate Max Howell portrayed a unique talent: 'Tubby resembled a gazelle or an antelope on the field, although one with a scrum helmet on, and it made him stand out. The spectators, and the selectors, could see that helmet bobbing up all over the field. Above all he was an exceptional athlete who covered the ground magnificently, being particularly devastating in cover defence.'

The dashing NSW centre played his first game for the Waratahs against the All Blacks in June 1947. Here he cuts inside a defender.

The Allan family were working class folk who moved from Bathurst to Sydney in the early 1930s. Trevor's father, Herbert 'Slab' Allan, was a First World War hero who was severely wounded in the Battle of Hamel and lived with embedded shrapnel for the rest of his life. His bravery was rewarded with the British Military Medal at Pozières and the French Médaille militaire at Bullecourt.

Trevor was a slightly chubby child and his two brothers liked to call him 'Fatty', hence his later nickname 'Tubby'. His first football steps were in rugby league at Willoughby Primary School where he starred in their all-conquering 5 stone 7 lb team. The introduction to rugby union came at secondary school at North Sydney Technical High where he represented in the NSW Combined High Schools first XV. His speed was honed on the athletics track and at 17 he claimed the Combined High Schools 440 yards title and chased home future Olympian John Treloar in the shorter sprints.

Tubby's raw talent had been spotted by the North Sydney rugby league club who saw him as a perfect fit for their code. But, fortuitously for rugby union, Trevor was raised in a 'father knows best' era. 'Slab' Allan decreed that his son's future was in rugby with the Gordon Highlanders. 'You're going to Gordon,' he's recorded as telling Trevor in the book *Wallaby Greats*. 'If you don't get big-headed and stupid, I can see you playing for Australia in the near future. You can forget about that if you go to league. There's no coming back. Go to Gordon and see how good you are.' Trevor's father never minced his words. He was a tough taskmaster and his prediction was accurate. Nevertheless, the rugby league scouts did not relent in making their persistent approaches over the next five years.

Trevor's rise through the rugby ranks was rapid and spectacular. Nine months after leaving North Sydney Technical High he found himself on a Sunderland flying boat departing Rose Bay for New Zealand as a brand new Wallaby. Just five weeks before his 20th birthday Allan pulled on the green Australian jumper for the first time against the powerful North Auckland side in Whangarei. 'It was a tremendous feeling,' he later recalled. 'I kept putting it on and taking it off. New Zealand

represented something I had not experienced before. It was a real rugby nation.'

The match was a fine spectacle with the home side winning 32-19 despite Australia's five-try haul. Trevor made a stunning debut in attack delivering the final pass for two of those tries and scoring one himself, as noted in *The Visitors* by Chester and McMillan. '[Arthur] Buchan led his forwards through and the ball came back to [Cyril] Burke, who sent his backs away. Allan beat Hook who had changed places with Johnny Smith, then swerved slightly infield. As Smith prepared to tackle him, Allan dummied to [Jim] Stone before sprinting on to score a glorious try after a run of 50 yards.'

Trevor missed the next five tour games with a fractured wrist but was rushed back into the national team for his Test debut in Dunedin where he continued his ferocious battle with Johnny Smith. It was a baptism of fire as the experienced Smith had emerged as the outstanding player in the excellent New Zealand Army side that toured Europe after the Second World War and played in the so-called 'Victory Internationals'. Australia lost both games against the Kiwis but were unlucky in the

Second Test at Eden Park going down 14-10 despite scoring two tries to one. Rookie centre Allan scored a try in the First Test and his speed, anticipation and never-say-die attitude in both matches stamped him as a player of rare class. The inexperienced tourists won respect and the opportunity to blood so many new players augured well for the major nine-month Wallaby tour of Britain, France, Canada and the United States, the following year.

The Kiwis retained the Bledisloe Cup in Sydney nine months later winning 27-14. Already, Allan's leadership potential was recognised when he was named vice-captain at just 20 years of age. Writing in *The Sydney Morning Herald* Tom Goodman highlighted his contribution. 'Trevor Allan was the brains of the Australian backline. He again showed himself a fine defensive player and was always dangerous in attack.'

When the tour party of 30 players was announced on ABC Radio in July 1947, Trevor was again named vice-captain – a remarkable vote of confidence for one so young and relatively inexperienced. Thousands of fans joined family and friends at No. 7 Wharf Woolloomooloo to send off their heroes who then spent six weeks aboard the *Orion* en route to England via Colombo and Aden. Those Wallabies were the first Australian sporting team to visit the United Kingdom after the Second World War. Following their arrival, the bus journey from Tilbury to London proved distressing as the tourists witnessed the devastation by the German bombings to so many buildings along the route.

Six games into the tour the Wallabies found themselves at Twickenham pitted against Combined Services. Late in the game disaster struck when skipper Bill McLean's leg snapped after being caught in a ruck. He would never play Test rugby again. In that fleeting moment Trevor Allan's tour was turned upside down. Five days beyond his 21st birthday, he was now the captain of the Third Wallabies, less than two years after graduating from high school. Suddenly he was leading men who had put their lives on the line and survived the horrors of war. Battle-hardened diggers such as gnarly Queensland prop 'Wallaby' Bob McMaster who'd fought in the bloody Tarakan Landing in the Borneo campaign two years earlier. The team also included RAAF airmen who had duelled with the Germans in the skies over Britain,

Trevor Allan was ABC Sport's rugby expert on television for 17 years. When Norman May retired in 1980 he was joined by the author.

and even a Changi POW survivor. Trevor's instinctive reaction was to lead by example, with humility and authority. After assisting the stretcher-bearers carry his stricken captain to the Twickenham sideline, Trevor returned to his silent and stunned teammates. As he made eye contact he said the following words: 'Let's get on with the job.' That they did.

Teammate Eric Tweedale paid Trevor the ultimate accolade in *Eric Tweedale: The Last of His Tribe* by Peter Fenton. 'Trevor was an absolutely magnificent player and a wonderful young fellow. He had all of us right behind him from the start and he proved to be an exceptional captain. Don't forget a lot of us

older men had come out of the services. Several were commissioned officers who knew what discipline was about and how important it was to success. We gave him total respect and he repaid us.'

The injured Bill McLean, who'd also seen active service in the war, remained with the team and was part of the leadership group behind the scenes. Indeed, in *A Life Worth Living* Nick Shehadie fondly recalled the occasion when the party visited Buckingham Palace. It was the highlight of the tour. 'Once inside we formed a half circle. King George VI and the Queen greeted us. Bill McLean escorted His Majesty to the reception area, and Arnold Tancred [manager] escorted the Queen. But all eyes were on Princess Margaret, escorted by Trevor Allan. Jeff Noseda the team secretary, accompanied Princess Elizabeth. The Royals had a word to say to each one of us, and we had an anxious moment, keeping our fingers crossed, when His Majesty met Phil Hardcastle, as both suffered from a speech impediment. Luckily all went well.'

The Australians won 25 of their 30 matches in Britain and Ireland and 9 of 10 in France. The victories over Scotland, Ireland .

and England were founded on defence. As testament to their defensive strength the Wallabies did not have their goal line crossed in the four home internationals. This was thanks, in no small part, to their new skipper's devastating tackling prowess. No single incident demonstrated this better than his incredible match-saver against England. The game was in the balance when winger David Swarbrick sprinted clear with no-one in front. In *Days Without Sunset* Denzil Batchelor waxed lyrical about Trevor's heroics. 'He

Fortress Eden Park in Auckland could not repel this dynamic duo of Immortals. Trevor's Wallabies won there in 1949 and Campo's team prevailed in 1986, as marked by Australia Post.

[Swarbrick] was indeed over the line, safely marvellously home. He had but to fall on his face and England would be a try up. And then as Swarbrick hurled himself down, a pin-pointed rocket caught him, swept him through mid-air, ball and all, into the no-man's-land of touch in goal. Nothing in the whole game can offer such a split-second quintessence of drama.'

But Australia was denied a grand slam against the four Home Nations by just two Welsh penalty goals. Wales downed the Wallabies 6-0 in a war of attrition at Cardiff Arms Park. The torrid defence on both sides nullified any attack to the extent that neither fullback was called on to make a single tackle. Australia missed two kicks in front from 30 metres and the lack of a reliable goal kicker arguably cost them victory. Hard statistics highlighted that vulnerability throughout the tour. The Wallabies scored 98 tries in Britain and Ireland but could manage only 36 conversions. The BBC later named Trevor as one of the three greatest rugby players to play in the British Isles in the first 50 years of the twentieth century.

The significance of the Wallabies' famous Bledisloe Cup series triumph in New Zealand in 1949 was downplayed in some quarters because the All Blacks already had 30 players in South Africa. What is often forgotten is that anyone with more than one-eighth Maori blood was banned from touring the republic. This meant the finest Maori players stayed at home. There were also several controversial omissions and consequently things did not fare well for the All Blacks in South Africa. They lost all four Tests which only reinforced the school of thought that many of their best players were still available to play at home against Australia.

In the First Test at Athletic Park in Wellington the Wallabies set up a match-winning lead of 11-0 at half-time after skipper Allan elected to run with the gale. With flankers Col Windon and Dave Brockhoff prominent, the All Blacks were tackled out of the game in the second half and the Wallabies emerged 11-6 winners. A 16-9 victory at Eden Park in the Second Test was achieved with similar conviction. The Australian forwards, led by Nick Shehadie and Rex Mossop, provided the platform for victory. Head-geared captain Trevor Allan was chaired

> 'Clutching the massive Bledisloe Cup in both hands, he raised it above his shoulders as the Kiwis came down the gangway.'

from the field by teammates in celebration of their first Bledisloe Cup triumph in 15 years. The Aussies had won 11 of the 12 tour matches. Their colourful coach 'Wild Bill' Cerutti, who had played in the losing Cup series in 1932, decided to seize the moment and was at the wharf in Sydney when the other All Blacks arrived back from South Africa. Clutching the massive Bledisloe Cup in both hands, he raised it above his shoulders as the Kiwis came down the gangway. In a cheeky gesture no doubt designed to entrench trans-Tasman rivalry he shouted, 'Here it is. It's ours now boys.'

At the time, rugby union still clung doggedly to its strict amateur traditions and rules. But for a working-class young man with marketable talent, those restrictions seemed unreasonable. After missing the twin Tests against the touring British and Irish Lions in 1950 through injury, 23-year-old Allan decided it was time for

a change. He agreed to switch to rugby league with English club Leeds but wanted no announcement until after his club season with Gordon had ended. But the excited player agent regrettably sent a cable from Sydney and suddenly the word was out. Allan withdrew from that deal but later accepted a massive offer for four years in the UK from the powerful Leigh rugby league club. He received a sign-on fee of £6,250 (tax free), a job, accommodation and match payments – plus return first-class fares by ship. For Allan it was better than winning the lottery. Tubby married his childhood sweetheart Judy Knuckey two days before departure aboard the *Orcades*.

In a controversial move, the unforgiving NSW Rugby Union then banned him from the code, a decision that was later reversed. Trevor played 97 games for Leigh scoring 52 tries. On his return to Sydney he was welcomed with open arms by the Gordon club and took over the first grade coaching reins in 1955. He then restarted his league career with North Sydney before retiring in 1958. Allan became an expert television commentator for the Australian Broadcasting Commission's rugby league coverage the following year and held that role until 1970 when he switched back to rugby as the ABC TV expert commentator. He continued in that role until 1986.

Following the capture of the Bledisloe Cup in 1949, the *New Zealand Rugby Almanack* paid him the highest praise: 'An extremely speedy and elusive centre, "Tubby" Allan puts every ounce of energy into his football. He achieves the almost impossible by being brilliant both on attack and in defence. Never stinting himself, Allan does the work of two men, his cover defence and backing up being outstanding. He is ever ready to open up an attack with one of his straight dashes upfield; often he has caught the defence on the wrong foot by a sudden change of direction, and flashed through to either score a try or make one possible.' Professor Max Howell, his teammate on that 1949 tour, had the final word: 'A boy prodigy, he became a man overnight with the responsibility of captaincy, and handled himself always with class and poise. No-one ever doubted his sincerity and commitment on the field of play.'

Simply the best. Former Wallaby coaches (left to right) Rod Macqueen, Dave Brockhoff, Bob Dwyer, Alan Jones and captains John Solomon and Trevor Allan were celebrated at a luncheon in 2005.

It was often said that John Thornett was born to lead – often by example. Here he is tackled by British Lion Ray McLoughlin in 1966.

Birthdate:	30 March 1935 (died 4 January 2019)
Place of birth:	Sydney, New South Wales
Nickname:	Thorn
Caps:	37 (Wallaby #410)

Revered as 'the captain's captain', the inspirational Thornett led the Wallabies in 63 matches including 16 Tests. He made his Test debut in 1955, aged 20, as a flanker against the All Blacks in Wellington. Four weeks later he was in the Australian side that beat New Zealand for only the second time at Eden Park in Auckland. After switching from lock to tight-head prop after the First Test defeat in South Africa in 1963 he led the Wallabies to their famous back-to-back victories in Cape Town and Johannesburg. His favourite win was the 6-3 defeat of the All Blacks in Christchurch in 1958 after the Wallabies had been written off by a Kiwi scribe as 'the worst team Australia has ever sent in any code'.

John Thornett was the eldest of three rugby-playing brothers who each ascended to rarefied status in the annals of Australian sport.

As the senior member of the trio, John is acknowledged as one of the greatest Wallaby captains in a Test career that spanned 13 seasons. During the 1960s his humble authoritative leadership style was integral to the resurgence of Australian rugby on the world stage.

Youngest brother Richard was a triple international who represented his country in rugby union, rugby league and water polo. Middle brother Ken played first grade for Randwick Rugby Club straight out of school before

Australian rugby's three musketeers: John (left), Ken and Dick. The three brothers all achieved 'hall of fame' status from their football exploits.

switching codes to become an Australian rugby league international and a member of that code's Hall of Fame.

They were an incredible sporting family. Alongside their rugby exploits the three boys all played water polo at elite level for the Bronte club in Sydney. John

was selected for the Melbourne Olympics but withdrew to focus on his blossoming rugby career which had already realised a Test debut against South Africa. Instead he opted to tour Japan with the Australian Universities rugby team. Richard made the Olympic team for Rome in 1960 and, although again unavailable, John underlined his quality with a spectacular five-goal haul for New South Wales against Western Australia in the National titles held in Melbourne. He was the team captain at Bronte and the three siblings were heavily involved in the club's run of four successive water polo state premierships from 1959 to 1962.

John's integrity and selfless leadership qualities were defined in the pool at an early age, but his true sporting destiny would emerge on dry land. Dux of the school at Sydney Boys' High, Thornett initially represented Sydney University where he studied Engineering. He debuted in first grade as an 18-year-old centre before switching to the back row. Club coach Barney Walsh immediately predicted his new recruit was destined to captain the Wallabies. John played in three straight premiership winning first grade sides for the students from 1953 to 1955 before joining his beloved Northern Suburbs. With established fellow-Wallabies Rod Phelps and Jim Cross, John was at the forefront of Norths' golden era which extended into the first half of the 1960s. Young players such as John 'Sparrow' Dowse, Les Austin and Roy Prosser all won their way into the Wallaby ranks on the back of Norths' dominant Shute Shield team.

Thornett's first experience of Test rugby came in 1955 against the All Blacks in Wellington. It was a classic baptism of fire. Selected at flanker alongside fellow back-rowers 'Mac' Hughes and Brian Johnson, he was one of Australia's best forwards in the 16-8 defeat. The All Blacks went on to clinch the Bledisloe Cup in the Second Test in Dunedin winning 8-0, but only after a last minute try by the flying Ron Jarden. Australia's 8-3 triumph in the Third Test then underlined the quality and tenacity of their newly sculpted scrum with the rejuvenated Hughes scoring one of Australia's tries. Authors Chester and McMillan wrote in *The Visitors* that 'the loose trio of Keith Cross, "Mac" Hughes and John Thornett were in devastating form'.

Yet three years later, in 1958, the Wallabies were dismissed as 'no-hopers' by one rugby writer on their arrival in New Zealand. They were still recovering from a winless record in all five Internationals in Britain, Ireland and France during the Australian spring and summer. Injured and unavailable for the seven-try drubbing in the First Test in Wellington, Thornett's recall for the return encounter was the only selection change. His back-row partners were the future international rugby league enforcer Kevin Ryan and new skipper, Charles 'Chilla' Wilson.

Australia's hero that day was 20-year-old Terry Curley whose towering performance ranks with the finest by any Wallaby fullback. His continued backline incursions rattled the Kiwis and his heroic defensive efforts in the second half all but sealed the improbable 6-3 victory. Thornett later recalled the elation of that triumph: 'We came off winners against all the forecasts of the experts and I can still remember the gleeful figures jumping up and down for joy on the top deck of the stand. They were the Australian reserves who had not played.' It is no surprise that this Second Test win over New Zealand in Christchurch was unquestionably the 'sweetest' victory of Thornett's distinguished career.

The beginning of a new decade heralded the arrival of a small army of fresh faces for the Wallabies. In 1961 John's brother Dick was one of 11 debutants picked for the First Test against Fiji. He played at No. 8 with new captain and scrum-half Ken Catchpole, and another future

triple international, winger Michael Cleary. For the Second Test at the SCG, John found himself selected at lock and the Thornett brothers packed down for the first of their nine Tests together. Australia was pushed hard by the flying Fijians but won all three Tests. The bevy of bold selections confirmed the emergence of an exciting new era for the national team.

Back on NZ soil in 1962 the reshaped Wallabies matched a powerful All Blacks' side led by legendary front-rower Wilson Whineray who played 77 matches for New Zealand including 68 as captain. John assumed the Wallaby captaincy from fullback Jim Lenehan for the First Test in Wellington and was joined by brother Dick for the second of their four Tests together as locking partners in the second row. The Australians endured an unlucky 9-9 draw. In the Second Test loss in Dunedin – by the dismal scoreline of 3-0 – the lone second-half penalty by NZ fullback colossus Don Clarke yielded the only points that separated the teams.

The Kiwis then claimed the Third Test in Auckland by 16-8 but rugby historians remember that match more for a remarkable coincidence than the result. The Kiwis selected Stan Meads to play alongside his brother Colin. That meant that two pairs of brothers were the opposing locks in the same match. Meanwhile, the blooding of NSW back-rower Peter 'Charlie' Crittle and dashing Queensland centre Dick Marks proved pivotal for the following international campaigns. Both made impressive debuts. (Richard Thornett switched to rugby league the following year and quickly made an impact as a mobile ball-playing forward. He joined brother Ken

Greg Davis heads downfield against South Africa in 1963, with Thornett and Peter Crittle in support.

The 1963 Wallabies were popular tourists in South Africa. Downtime in Cape Town was a perfect diversion from the intense rugby battlefields.

on the 1963–64 Kangaroo tour of Great Britain and France. That side also contained ex-Wallabies Michael Cleary, Jim Lisle, Arthur Summons and Kevin Ryan.)

Emerging from the tough 1962 Bledisloe Cup series, John Thornett's young Wallabies were now splendidly match hardened for rugby's ultimate challenge: an away series against South Africa. They would be centre stage in a sporting theatre where even the All Blacks had always fallen short. The Wallaby battle cry was '*Operation Die Bokke*'. Their mission: to take down the mighty Springboks in South Africa over four Test matches – including two that would be played at altitude.

Armed with valuable lessons from the torrid 1961 short tour of South Africa, the Australians adopted a strategy to fatigue their bigger opponents. The more mobile, bulked-up Wallaby pack was complemented by a pacey disruptive back row and a skilful, speedy backline. This blueprint had been developed directly from the Second Test loss in Port Elizabeth in 1961 when, although beaten 23-11 after being outmuscled in earlier games, the Wallaby forwards competed hard and won respect in a free-flowing contest. On returning home from that tour Thornett and Heming took to the weights room adding considerable bulk and strength to their frames. John gained an extra stone while Rob could soon clap his hands above the goalpost crossbar from a standing jump. '*Operation Die Bokke*' was ready for execution.

Prior to departure John gained his first big scalp as skipper when the Wallabies downed England in the mud at the SCG by 18-9. It was also Australia's first win over a major rugby nation on home soil for 29 years.

After losing the turgid First Test in Pretoria by 14-3, Australia made seven positional changes for the next international to be played a month later in Cape Town. Skipper Thornett changed position yet again – this time from lock to tight-head prop. Crittle and Heming were installed as the new locks to address the astonishing 29-12 lineout deficit and also to boost mobility and agility in the forwards. Debutant Jules 'Vodka' Guerassimoff joined fellow terrier Greg Davis to set up a mini 'bomb squad' in the back row. Catchpole replaced Ken McMullen at scrum-half and Marks was reinstated to the three-quarter line on the wing.

It worked. The Wallabies levelled the series with a thrilling 9-5 victory in front of 34,000 fans. Near half-time Catchpole worked the blindside for a crucial try by winger Jim Boyce. Exciting newcomer Phil Hawthorne followed up with a neat drop goal and a superb try-saving tackle on imperious SA centre

John Gainsford to help secure the win. That result was founded on Australia's upbeat tempo, solid set piece and fierce tackling, especially by flankers Davis and Guerassimoff on the Springbok inside backs. Catchpole and Hawthorne, working in concert, were supreme conductors for their highly motivated forward pack.

Local sportswriter A.C. Parker wrote of that match: 'Nothing can detract from the magnificence of Australia's team effort. Davis and Catchpole had a decisive influence on the result – the New Zealand born breakaway for the destructive havoc he created among the Springbok inside backs and the scrum-half for his masterly dictation of play from behind.'

Two weeks later, Ellis Park – 1,753 metres above sea level – would prove a watershed for Australian Rugby. No Australian team had won at that ground. With 65,000 South Africans cheering on their team the Wallabies prevailed by 11-9. Fullback Terry Casey was the match winner with a conversion from touch, a penalty goal and an amazing 40-metre drop goal. Australia's lone try was a classic. Heming tapped a lineout throw to Crittle who veered infield and delivered a magical delayed pass to Marks who burst clear before delivering a precision pass to John Williams. The flying winger left five desperate defenders in his wake on a blistering sprint to the corner. Williams' sheer pace came as no surprise to the Australians as he'd been selected as a sprinter in the national track squad for the Empire and Commonwealth Games in Perth the previous year.

In a fine gesture of sportsmanship, the defeated Springbok forwards carried Thornett off the field on their shoulders. In *A Dangerous Breed* by Mike Jenkinson, centre Dick Marks recalled how impressed he was by those South African players: 'Along with the Welsh crowd singing "Waltzing Matilda" after we beat their team for the first time in history at Cardiff Arms Park in '66, this was the most memorable instance of sportsmanship in my career.'

Despite losing the Fourth Test in Port Elizabeth, John Thornett's 1963 team had squared the series against all odds. Those Wallabies still rank among Australia's greatest tourists, inflicting back-to-back home losses on the Boks for the first time since 1896. On their return home they were afforded a ticker tape parade along George Street in downtown Sydney. The 20,000-strong lunchtime crowd celebrated their brave, free-spirited campaign.

The Wallaby front row of Thornett, Peter Johnson and Jon White, which had performed so well in South Africa, was now firmly established as a world-class unit. In 1965 the fearless trio provided a powerful platform for twin victories over South Africa who were in transit to New Zealand. An 18-11 win at the SCG was followed by a rain-affected 12-8 score at Lang Park in Brisbane. Skipper Thornett was chaired from the field by his exhausted teammates. It was his first series win as captain, in his 34th Test. This made him the new cap record-holder, passing Tony Miller.

John undertook his final Wallaby tour in 1966–67 to Britain, Ireland, France and Canada, his fourth as captain and eighth overall. But there would be no fairytale finale to his distinguished career. He unluckily contracted impetigo when packing down in a scrum against a pig farmer in Leicester. The skin disease kept him out of all four games against the Home Nations including the wins over Wales and England. The infection was so contagious that Thornett was not allowed to train with the team and

Thornett funnels the ball back to Ken Catchpole against the Boks at the SCG in 1965.

had to wear a plastic bag over his head when in contact with his fellow tourists. Then, when his condition finally improved, he elected to drop himself for the Welsh Test. Teammate Alan Cardy commented: 'At that moment he showed us that he was not only a great leader but also a great gentleman.'

Thornett returned as skipper against the Barbarians at Cardiff Arms Park and led the side to a first-ever win over the famous club. As he was chaired from the field the vast crowd spontaneously burst into a rendition of 'Waltzing Matilda'.

'Thorn' also played in the final Test against France but although the Wallabies scored two tries to one, Australia lost 20-14. Then, at 32, the veteran skipper called time on his decorated career. Fittingly, his 37 caps and 114 matches were a record haul for his country.

John Thornett was born to lead. On and off the field, his commander-in-chief role within the Wallaby family was always discharged with his distinctive class, skill and humanity. World Cup-winning coach Bob Dwyer credits the Thornett era as the reason the

Thornett the farmer. A portrait by his Wallaby teammate John Williams.

Wallabies eventually rose to such heights more than two decades later. Following the 1966–67 European tour, manager Bill McLaughlin set up the first coach education panel headed by Dick Marks. Peter Crittle was the chairman and the other panel members included Thornett, prop John Freedman, hooker Peter Johnson and Wallabies coach Dave Brockhoff. Dwyer recalls their impact: 'For me, nothing before or since has been more important to Australian Rugby than the establishment of our first ever coaching panel under Dick Marks. Our subsequent elevation to number one team in the world was a direct impact of the coaching panel and all those wonderful players in the John Thornett era.'

John was one of five inaugural inductees into the Wallabies Hall of Fame and subsequently was an inductee to the World Rugby Hall of Fame. He eventually moved onto the land and farmed in Cowra before settling on the far South Coast of NSW. He adored the bush and the country lifestyle. He also continued to serve in honorary roles in administration and coaching. John's focus on the spirit of the game was always front and centre on the rugby pitch. In *A Dangerous Breed* by Mike

'John was one of five inaugural inductees into the Wallabies Hall of Fame and subsequently was an inductee to the World Rugby Hall of Fame.'

Jenkinson, which focused on a return visit to South Africa by the celebrated 1963 Wallaby tourists, the author described Thornett's appeal both as a player and person: 'Thornett, handsome, unassuming and with Engineering and Science degrees from Sydney University led by quiet example. His good looks, charm and on-field skills gave him film star status in South Africa. He handled his public speaking and media liaison duties with unfailing modesty and good humour.'

Even today in the professional era, the thrust of John Thornett's well-documented philosophy has stood the test of time. He expressed that ethos in these words: 'Those who play must always uphold the highest standards of sportsmanship. The amateur spirit is a state of mind about how you approach a match in the field.'

Scrum-half Ken Catchpole during training at Finsbury Square, London, in 1966,

4

KEN CATCHPOLE

Birthdate:	21 June 1939 (died 21 December 2017)
Place of birth:	Sydney, New South Wales
Nickname:	Catchy
Caps:	27 (Wallaby #455)

Catchpole was a true rugby genius and warrants consideration as Australia's greatest ever player. He made his representative debut as a 19-year-old scrum-half for NSW against the 1959 British Lions. At 21 he won his first Wallaby cap and was also named captain against Fiji in Brisbane. Five weeks later 'Catchy' was selected as captain/coach of the 1961 Wallaby touring team to South Africa. In 1963 he starred in the historic drawn Test series in South Africa. His celebrated eight-year Test career was prematurely terminated at just 28 after he suffered a shocking leg injury against the All Blacks at the SCG.

Ken Catchpole was a unique talent according to World Cup-winning Wallaby coach Bob Dwyer: 'He was so much better than everyone else. It was almost as though he was playing on another level.'

In an era when Australia often struggled to match the elite nations in the pitched forward battles, his ability to turn ugly possession from his pack into quality ball for his backline set him apart.

Catchpole's start in life was far from auspicious. His first 11 months were spent in hospital suffering from eczema and asthma. Later, to build up his chest and lung capacity, his parents involved him in swimming and athletics where the natural sporting ability of their youngster soon emerged. He began playing rugby union at Coogee

A lightning clearance from the maestro.

Preparatory School as a 10-year-old. While Ken also excelled at swimming, tennis, cricket and sport in general, his parents encouraged a strong focus on his school studies and self-expression. That strategy was rewarded handsomely when he earned an academic scholarship to Scots College, one of Sydney's famed Great Public Schools.

Not surprisingly, at such a notable rugby nursery, rugby was soon front-and-centre for young Catchpole, even above his favourite sport of tennis and winning the 880 yards GPS championship. Although

beginning as an inside-centre, his future at scrum-half was quickly recognised and he spent three years in that role for the first XV. He also took up refereeing at 15 and continued officiating through his remaining high-school years. It was clear that Catchpole's potential as a unique rugby talent was firmly on notice.

In Theo Clark's splendid video documentary *Sometimes the Best Ever*, which celebrates the 50th anniversary of the 1966–67 Wallabies, Bob Dwyer recounts an astonishing exchange between two members of the immortal 1927–28 Waratahs in Catchy's last year of high school: 'Wally Meagher and Cyril Towers were great Randwick rugby men and extraordinary judges of player talent. Wally told me he asked Cyril to come and have a look at a player from Scots College in a pre-season trial match in 1957 because he thought the youngster may just become "the greatest scrum-half the world has ever seen".'

The fact that these two veteran Wallabies could recognise sheer talent in a mere schoolboy rugby player gives the lie to the German philosopher Schopenhauer's famous contention that 'genius reaches a target no-one else can see'.

Catchpole won a scholarship to Sydney University where he undertook a science degree, gaining honours in chemistry. That professional qualification secured him work in the food industry, first with Davis Gelatine and later as marketing manager for the Meadow Lea group.

In 1958 Meagher and Towers registered Ken with Randwick Colts and the following season he was picked in first grade. After a handful of games in the top grade, the representative selectors then pitchforked him into the NSW team to meet the British Lions at the Sydney Sports Ground. The celebrated visitors were en route to New Zealand where they eventually won 20 of 25 matches including the Fourth Test against the All Blacks at Eden Park. The Waratahs stunned the Lions winning by 18-14 and the 19-year-old Catchpole celebrated with a debut try against the visitors.

A Test debut had to wait until 1961 after incumbent Wallaby scrum-half Des Connor decided to pursue his teaching aspirations in New Zealand. Remarkably, Connor was quickly appointed vice-captain of the All Blacks, going on to win 12 caps. The Australian selectors responded swiftly. Catchy was named captain in his first Test against Fiji and, incredibly, was then saddled with the additional responsibility of captain/coach for the short tour of South Africa. All this at the tender age of 21.

The Wallabies were well beaten in both Tests against the Springboks and it came as no surprise that Catchy was relieved of the captaincy burden the following year after an injury-strewn season. That decision prompted the beginning of John Thornett's memorable reign as Wallaby skipper over the next six years.

The 1963 Wallaby tour of South Africa ranks alongside the great Australian overseas rugby campaigns. At the time, the Springboks could rightly claim to be unofficial world champions after an unbeaten run in their 14 previous Tests, including two against the All Blacks and four against the touring British Lions. The Boks had also just completed a successful grand slam campaign in Europe. They were formidable.

Australia's 30-strong party was largely inexperienced and dominated by NSW players. Just four Queenslanders made the squad. One of those was young centre, Dick Marks, who identified the four critical Wallaby performers. Twin flankers Jules Guerassimoff and Greg Davis were singled out for their devastating offensive assault on the South African inside backs, wreaking havoc throughout the Test series. In *A Dangerous Breed* by Mike Jenkinson, Marks also highlighted the immense contribution of a spring-heeled lineout exponent Rob Heming. But his highest praise was reserved for Australia's mercurial scrum-half: 'On the playing field, we had one definite superstar in the most important position of all, scrum-half. A diminutive man, Ken

Catchpole had lightning reflexes, an exceptional burst of speed and a very good rugby brain. With a highly promising player, [Phil] Hawthorne, outside Catchpole it was reasonable to expect that we would have an advantage in the halves, which would be a great creative hub.'

The Wallabies lost the First Test in Pretoria by 14-3 in front of 52,000, hamstrung by a lack of possession, especially in the lineout battle where South Africa enjoyed a dominant advantage. Australian manager Bill McLaughlin agreed the best side had won but was confident the result could be overturned four weeks later in Cape Town.

Australia made wholesale changes for the critical showdown. Catchpole returned from an arm injury, skipper Thornett moved to the front row and Heming and Peter Crittle were united for the first time in the second row. Flanker Guerassimoff made his debut in the back row and Terry Casey came in for Peter Ryan at fullback while Ian Moutray and Marks were additions to the three-quarter line. The new personnel made telling contributions. The revamped forward pack held its own against their much larger opponents and the Catchpole-led backline proved superior in front

One of Catchpole's greatest performances came the day Australia scored a famous 23-11 win over England at Twickenham in 1967.

of the 34,000 strong crowd. Local newspaper *The Argus* noted: 'The Wallabies' 9-5 victory is scored completely on their own merits.'

With the series now level, selectors made only one change for the Third Test in Johannesburg. Flying winger Johnny Williams had recovered from bronchitis allowing Marks to move into the centre. It shaped as the ultimate challenge – a wounded Springbok side, set to dominate in the rarefied altitude of Ellis Park, secure in the knowledge the Wallabies had never won a Test at the famous ground.

The expected 65,000 parochial fans all knew that no touring team had won successive Tests against the Boks since 1896. The Aussies were huge underdogs and the outcome shaped as a foregone conclusion.

Against all odds Australia prevailed in an epic contest by 11-9. The special hero of the day was fullback Casey with a match-winning dropped goal, penalty and conversion. Williams' scintillating finish to score the only Wallaby try was a heart-stopper – he evaded five would-be tacklers with his lethal turn of foot.

'Catchy' scores for Randwick in the 1967 grand final against Gordon at the Sydney Sports Ground. The sixties were a golden era for the Galloping Greens.

In the biography *Until the Final Whistle* by Mike Jenkinson, Phil Hawthorne expressed his awe at the inspired efforts of his teammates: 'Terry Casey was super at fullback that day. His dropped goal just seemed to go on and on through the rarefied atmosphere. The forwards were magnificent and Catchy had one of his greatest tests. We had made Australian rugby history.'

John Thornett's Wallabies had become the first touring team to beat the Springboks in consecutive Tests in the 20th century. Although South Africa squared the series in

the Fourth Test in Port Elizabeth winning 22-16, Australia's magnificent African campaign was acclaimed throughout the rugby world. All up, the team played 24 matches, recording 15 wins and a draw with eight losses. In *The Springboks* A.C. Parker wrote: 'Catchpole with his razor-sharp reflexes and cat-like quickness in everything he did, had a superlative tour and was undoubtedly the world's best scrum-half at this stage.'

Fresh from their heroic efforts the Wallabies shaped up for an eagerly anticipated series against the All Blacks in New Zealand in 1964. The home team had just completed a long tour of Britain and France winning 34 of their 36 matches. The Kiwis won the First Test in Dunedin by 14-9, both sides scoring a try, but fullback Mick Williment's dropped goal and conversion proved the difference. The Wallaby forwards held their own against a surprisingly subdued home pack.

New Zealand convincingly won the Second Test which meant the Third Test in Wellington a week later was a dead rubber. No-one told the Wallabies. Their form reversal was astonishing. The All Blacks were beaten upfront by an inspired Aussie pack. Davis and Guerassimoff rattled their inside backs while Catchpole and Hawthorne orchestrated the attack with brilliance and precision. Stewart Boyce scored two tries, Hawthorne kicked a 40-yard dropped goal and Casey kicked three penalties The final score of 20-5 was the largest defeat of an All Black team against Australia and the second heaviest defeat against all comers. Essentially, the Wallabies fielded the same side that had downed the Springboks at Ellis Park twelve months earlier. The only additions were try scorer Boyce and No. 8 David Shepherd from Victoria. The *NZ Rugby Almanack* reported: 'By the time of the Third Test the tackling had improved, supported by clever play from halfback Catchpole, New Zealand at Wellington were forced to submit to the forward domination of an Australian pack that never let up. It was a great victory for Australia.'

Catchy's marvellous combination with Hawthorne extended to a record 17 Tests including the twin victories in 1965 over South Africa in Sydney and Brisbane. At the end of that year a South African newspaper named the pair in a World XV along with Greg Davis, Jon White and Peter Johnson. Australian rugby was at the top of the pile.

The 1966–67 tour of Britain, Ireland and France saw Catchpole reinstated as captain after John Thornett contracted impetigo in a scrum engagement. The Wallabies downed Wales and England but lost to Scotland, Ireland and France. The victory over England at Twickenham was the tour highlight. With Jim Lenehan at fullback and exciting newcomer John Brass joining the experienced Marks in the centres, the Wallaby backs dazzled. Hawthorne kicked three drop goals while Brass and Catchpole each scored super-slick tries. Poignantly, 10 years after Wally Meagher's assertion about a certain teenage Scots College scrum-half, the prophecy was fulfilled.

At the post-Test dinner, the president of the Rugby Football Union, Duggie Harrison, did not hold back in his praise for the Australian victory, saying: 'I have enjoyed immensely the refreshing brand of

'Catchpole with his razor-sharp reflexes and cat-like quickness in everything he did, had a superlative tour and was undoubtedly the world's best scrum-half at this stage.'

football they have played, particularly what they showed us today. It has also been my pleasure to see the greatest scrum-half the world has ever known.'

Ken Catchpole's distinguished Test career came to a shuddering halt on 15 June 1968 at the SCG. It was a moment that is engraved in the memories of anyone who was at the ground or saw the incident on television. New Zealand held a 19-3 lead nine minutes before half-time when the Wallaby captain found himself pinned in a ruck with one leg submerged under a bevy of bodies. Catchpole's free leg was soon in the massive hands of All Black legend Colin Meads. The giant lock tried to wrench Catchpole from the melee, stretching the scrum-half's muscles beyond breaking point. The result was horrific damage to his hamstring, groin and sciatic nerve. Catchpole would never play representative rugby again.

Catchy always dismissed suggestions that Meads had deliberately seized the moment to inflict serious damage. Instead, he believed that 'it was more of a silly accident and a stupid thing to do'. A repentant Meads said he was merely trying to move his opponent out of the way so he could ruck the ball back.

Over the next four years Ken gradually worked his way back to an acceptable level of fitness at club level and was able to play first grade again for Randwick, spearheading them to a premiership victory before announcing his retirement. He later became an extremely popular pundit for the Australian Broadcasting Commission's rugby union radio coverage, a long-serving member of the SCG Trust and was elected president of the New South Wales Rugby Union.

Catchy first met his second wife June, an art teacher, when she invited him to sit for his portrait. (At that stage June knew so little about sport she thought he was a famous cricketer.) Ken reluctantly agreed but when he arrived at her studio it was love at first sight. That portrait failed to win the Archibald Prize but the marriage it triggered lasted 40 happy years.

A sample of peer respect for Catchpole reveals useful insights into the man and the player. John Brass recalls his first match with Ken at Randwick. 'He asked me if I wanted the ball lace up or lace down? I was a young kid and couldn't believe someone could play to that level.' Wallaby fullback Peter Ryan fondly recalls the

Catchpole and ARU managing director John O'Neill unveil the bronze sculpture of Ken at the Sydney Football Stadium in 2010.

Catchpole magic. 'His captaincy and leadership were all by example. We didn't want to let him down because he was doing so much great stuff on the field.'

Rival New Zealand halfback Chris Laidlaw in his autobiography *Mud in Your Eye* encapsulated Ken's stature from an opponent's standpoint. 'As the supreme exponent of all the skills, Catchpole stands beyond rivalry. He was years ahead of his time. His pass was never long. It was, however, phenomenally fast and his technique of delivery perfect – just a flash of light to his fly-half.'

His twilight years were clouded by the relentless onset of dementia. At Wallaby reunions, at the insistence of his former teammates, he took great delight in reading aloud the feats of 'Ken Catchpole', often chuckling at a try-saving tackle or a searing break to set up a try. The tragedy was that he could read those accounts of his own exploits yet could not recall them.

Catchy died in 2017 at the age of 78. He had six children, one of whom Mark – a robust scrum-half – toured Canada and France with the 1993 Wallabies. A bronze statue of Catchpole delivering one of his trademark low-trajectory bullet passes sits outside Allianz Stadium in Sydney.

Simon Poidevin played 96 games for Australia including 59 Tests. He helped unravel the All Black myth.

5

SIMON POIDEVIN

Birthdate:	31 October 1958
Place of birth:	Goulburn, New South Wales
Nickname:	Poido
Caps:	59 (Wallaby # 614)

Simon Poidevin was famous for his physicality and abrasive approach. A tough, fearless and uncompromising loose forward, he was Australia's auburn-haired gladiator at the heart of the Wallabies' golden run in the 1980s and early 1990s. Raised on the family sheep and cattle farm, Braemar, on the outskirts of Goulburn, Poidevin relished his many pitched battles against All Black forward packs and won universal respect for his hard-nosed aggression and perpetual motion. He inspired and galvanised teammates, always leading by example.

One of five children, Simon Poidevin's rural heritage was ingrained in the rolling pastures of the southern tablelands of New South Wales. Generations of Poidevins worked the land surrounding Goulburn, Australia's oldest inland city, and sport was integral to their way of life. His grandfather, Les Hannan, was an outstanding centre who was selected for the first Wallaby tour of Britain in 1908 but broke his leg before departure and missed the trip of a lifetime. His grandson would triumphantly overturn that family misfortune 73 years later by winning selection for the 1981–82 Wallaby tour of Great Britain and Ireland.

Simon's rugged upbringing on the land equipped him brilliantly for contact sport. His early football experience was confined to rugby league at St Patrick's Primary School and his ultra-competitive instincts sometimes got out of hand. On

First year out of school and a premiership with the Goulburn Dirty Reds. Simon is centre back row.

one occasion in the under 10s he was given his marching orders after a 'tiff' with an opponent. In *Simon Poidevin: For Love Not Money*, he sheepishly recalled that unacceptable lapse. 'I don't know that I've ever been quite as upset about any incident on the field as I was about that. Mum and Dad weren't too happy either and must have wondered what sort of wild man they were rearing.'

Rugby league was replaced by union when Poidevin began high school at St Patrick's College, Goulburn. That switch proved a life-changing experience. Senior teacher Brother Powell was the school's rugby guru and coach of the first XV. His superior technical knowledge and all-consuming focus on discipline and hard work were legendary. St Patrick's was a rugby

powerhouse and a feisty young flanker named Simon Poidevin was hell bent on making the top side at any cost. That opportunity arrived in his penultimate year and those two seasons proved the making of the man. Selection in the ACT Schoolboys followed where he found himself opposing future Wallaby teammates including Steve Williams, Chris Roche and the future King of Rugby League, Wally Lewis. Simon was then chosen in the Australian Schools' side ensuring the flame-haired country tyro from Goulburn was suddenly on the radar of more senior and influential rugby figures.

Following a year of labouring with a concreter and a premiership with the Goulburn Dirty Reds, Simon decided to head to the 'big smoke' to enhance his rugby and professional career aspirations. In 1979 he enrolled at the University of NSW to study for a bachelor's course in wool and pastoral science. The UNSW rugby team played in the premier Shute Shield competition and in his second season the 20-year-old appeared in a Test curtain-raiser at Ballymore in Brisbane for the NSW Under 23 side against their Queensland counterparts.

Selection in the NSW senior team for the annual interstate clash with

Queensland then took his playing experience to a new level. At the T.G. Milner Field in suburban Sydney the Maroon forwards made a point of dishing out an appropriate initiation for the young newcomer. He came off second best against a celebrated international back row of Tony Shaw, Mark Loane and Greg Cornelsen. Simon remembers that 24-3 loss as one of the hardest games of rugby he had ever played. 'After the final whistle, as we were walking off, I felt like I'd just spent 80 minutes in a medieval torture chamber, either being stretched on the rack or dangling from the wall in chains. Hardly a bone in my entire body wasn't aching and I was bleeding from a dozen scrapes and cuts.' So fierce was the rucking that both his socks had been ripped to shreds. 'I'd just been to war.' But importantly he did not take a backward step and relished the opportunity to impose his strength in a match played at Test match ferocity. The point was taken by the Australian selectors.

Simon's big moment arrived in 1980 on the short tour of Fiji. He was named in the No. 6 jumper and was one of seven debutants for the one-off Test match. Australia won a grinding encounter 22-9 but far greater challenges loomed for the three contests against the All Blacks. Australia had regained the famed Bledisloe Cup (symbol of trans-Tasman superiority) the previous year at the SCG and was aiming to achieve a third straight victory over the Men in Black.

In a selection masterstroke, Australian coach Bob Templeton decided it was time to blood Mark Ella at fly-half and the newly created axis with former Australian Schools' teammates Michael Hawker and Michael O'Connor proved mesmerising. The Wallabies clinched the series in the Third Test at the SCG with a record 26-10 victory. Four wins from the last five clashes had surely debunked the public's perception of All Blacks invincibility once and for all. 'In my first season of international rugby, it was a dream start to my career,' Poidevin recalled. 'After succumbing for generations to All Black forward power, it looked like we had at last found a pack of our own to complement the marvellous backs that Australia always seems to produce year in and year out.'

The 1981–82 Wallaby tour of Britain was tipped to be a crowning experience for the newly-revamped Wallabies but a failure to kick their goals was a major factor in that campaign of lost dreams. Pre-tour predictions of a grand slam against the four Home Nations only added unnecessary pressure. A lone win over Ireland was probably more frustrating than disappointing because Australia had failed to close out the three losses when in a position to do so. Simon was an indispensable member of the Wallaby back row in all four Tests alongside Cornelsen and Loane with skipper Shaw shifted to lock. Poidevin reflected, 'We never really got going. Although Tony Shaw's men finished with 16 wins and 1 draw from 23 matches, we've got to live with the fact that history still judges us to be failures.'

Simon renewed his fierce rivalry with All Black flanker Mark 'Cowboy' Shaw (also known as 'The Manawatu Meatworker') later that year in New Zealand. New national coach Bob Dwyer was left stranded when nine experienced Queensland Wallabies made themselves unavailable for the tour. Dwyer cast a wide net that enabled the introduction of teenage wing sensation David Campese as one of a dozen new faces. Mark Ella became Australia's captain replacing Mark Loane and the Wallabies subsequently produced one of their greatest victories in the Second Test in Wellington when defending a 19-3 half-time lead into a force 7 gale.

Poidevin recalls the feverish mindset of every Wallaby player that day. 'In the first 30 seconds of the game Mark Shaw came at us; Rochey hit him low, I crunched him high, and we smashed him to the ground. Even now I can recall the questioning look on his face as if he didn't believe it. But the whole team had a huge roll on from the outset.' With 30 seconds remaining and the Wallabies clinging to a 19-16 lead, Simon vividly remembers the moment he dived on a loose ball near the Aussie goal line, supported by fellow back-rower Peter Lucas. The All Black forwards then proceeded to ruck the pair with the ruthless precision of a combine harvester. 'They were dancing up and down my back. But we knew if the ball went back our way we'd win the Test, and when Luco and I saw it heading back our side we actually started laughing with joy.' It was a combination of bravery and madness that summed up the situation – and indeed reflected Simon's rugby DNA.

Poidevin's decorated career featured three absolute standout Wallaby campaigns starting with the 1984 Grand Slam, followed by the 1986 Bledisloe Cup series win in New Zealand and then finally the 1991 Rugby World Cup triumph. The '84 'Slam' triggered a highly productive era under the indefatigable coaching of Alan Jones and his wonderful forwards guru Alec Evans. That historic clean sweep was constructed on the broad shoulders of a massive forward pack that could dominate the set-piece and any opposition. That powerful platform allowed instinctive playmaker Mark Ella to call the shots and ignite the match-winning skills of backs including Campese, Roger Gould and Nick Farr-Jones.

The template was supported by an unbreakable unity of purpose skilfully overseen by Jones and his small management team and on-field captain Andrew Slack. 'It was easily the best rugby team I'd ever been associated with (to that point),' Simon said. 'Four years beforehand when we won the Bledisloe Cup we had some fantastic backs, but for a complete team from front to back, this outfit was almost faultless. There was nothing they couldn't do. We also had Jonesy: the ultimate coach,

Poidevin scored his first Test try against France in 1981 at Ballymore. Australia won 17-15.

an absolute workhorse, extremely smart, able to get his message across and with an extraordinary ability to read players' moods and know precisely when to increase or ease the workload.'

Australia had never won a three-Test series on Kiwi soil but that all changed two years later in

1986. Most of New Zealand's best players had taken part in the controversial 'Cavaliers' tour of South Africa and were ineligible for the First Test in Wellington. The Wallabies scrambled home against the so-called 'Baby Blacks' by 13-12 but braced for a full backlash with the return of the suspended Cavaliers for the Second Test in Dunedin where Australia had been winless since 1903. The underdog Wallabies were controversially denied a series victory when Steve Tuynman appeared to have scored the match-winner only to be denied by Welsh referee Derek Bevan. He ruled 'too many hands on the ball'. Simon was adamant that Tuynman had forced the ball underneath his body. '(Bevan) wasn't in the ideal position to see what happened … most of the All Blacks even thought it was a try.'

Enrique Rodriguez, Simon Poidevin, Mick Murray receive instructions from coach Alan Jones at a training session in 1986.

New Zealand uncharacteristically resorted to a frantic running approach in the Eden Park decider and only desperate gallantry held them out in the first half. Simon was surprised by the tactic. 'As we chased and tackled from one side of the field to the other it crossed my mind how grateful I was for all the gruelling training Jonesy had put into us early in the tour.' The Wallabies prevailed by 22-9 after Campese scored the clincher in the dying stages. 'To me (the win) was more satisfying and even greater than the Grand Slam success in Britain.'

The inaugural Rugby World Cup in 1987 proved a major disappointment for Alan Jones' Wallabies who bowed out of contention when they lost to France in the semi-final at Sydney's Concord Oval. The chance to repeat their Eden Park glory the previous year was thwarted by a last-minute Serge Blanco try. But there was some consolation for Poidevin later that year when Jones named him Wallaby captain for the tour of Argentina. Australia drew 19-19 in the First Test but a hand injury forced Simon out of the Second Test loss which proved to be the last hurrah for Jones as Wallaby coach.

'When we won the Bledisloe Cup we had some fantastic backs, but for a complete team from front to back, this outfit was almost faultless.'

Bob Dwyer was appointed for a second stint as national coach in 1988. Initially, that prompted Poidevin to announce his retirement from Test rugby when told he'd been replaced as Wallaby captain by Nick Farr-Jones. But ironically it was a club game for his beloved Randwick that motivated him to reverse his call just 42 days later. The Galloping Greens played the All Blacks at Coogee Oval in what can only be described as an incredible spectacle. Nearly 10,000 fans crammed into the small seaside ground. The gates were closed half an hour before kick-off. Spectators climbed trees outside to watch the historic occasion. Poidevin had a running battle with New Zealand skipper Buck Shelford and his Randwick teammates that afternoon included Campese, Eddie Jones and Michael Cheika. The locals pushed the Kiwis to the wire playing well above themselves in a very physical contest. So,

Poidevin is a picture of concentration during Australia's 12-6 World Cup final victory over England at Twickenham in 1991.

when an SOS due to injuries came from Dwyer for the upcoming Bledisloe Cup series, the red-haired warrior just couldn't resist.

Simon was unavailable for Test duty in 1990 due to work commitments but a superb unbeaten run with the NSW Waratahs the following year under Rod Macqueen reaffirmed his desire to atone for the disappointment of 1987 and lift the Webb Ellis Cup at Twickenham. Reflecting on the great escape against Ireland in the quarter-final, Simon reckoned the subsequent extra week in Dublin preparing for the All Blacks was a blessing. 'The moment the whistle finally sounded for full-time at 19-18 all those Irish fans immediately transferred their loyalty and support from their own team to us.' His praise for Randwick teammate David Campese in the semi-final against New Zealand was unrestrained. 'In the sixth minute he scored the most exhilarating solo try of the tournament, and later created an even better team try, to show he was the best attacking player in the world and definitely the star performer in the World Cup.' Almost three weeks after Australia's thrilling 12-6 win over England in the final, Simon found himself in the middle of a ticker tape parade in Sydney. 'George Street was chock-a-block with thousands of people … they all simply wanted to help celebrate the greatest team achievement ever by Australia in a truly international sport and be part of rugby's finest hour in this country. Bob Dwyer was the chief architect of our Rugby World Cup triumph. He provided innovation, exact and demanding physical preparation, emotional intelligence and an incredible coaching IQ.'

Simon reached managing director status with global giant Citibank in a financial services career spanning nearly four decades. He captained Australia in four Tests and played 96 games for the Wallabies including 59 Tests across 13 seasons. He was capped on 58 occasions for the NSW Waratahs. 'Poido' joined the Randwick Club in 1982 and was a member of eight premiership-winning teams over 11 seasons.

In the twilight of Simon's Wallaby career the doyen of NZ rugby writers D.J. Cameron gave a Kiwi appraisal of the ginger-haired tyro from across the 'Ditch'. 'They should wrap him in his Wallaby No. 6, lead him quietly back to Randwick, put a middy in his hand, and never let any other Wallaby wear that number. And there Poidevin would stay. Content. Until he heard men in black jerseys going "kamate, kamate". And then Poidevin would be off to battle again.'

Simon and his wife Robin reside at Coogee Beach and have three sport obsessed sons. Christian plays professional rugby for San Diego, Jean-Luc is a National League Water Polo player with UNSW/Wests and youngest Gabe graduated from Randwick's Colts with a premiership.

The Randwick and Wallaby great sets the pace for Randwick's Junior Academy members in Sydney's Wanda Beach sandhills.

Mark Ella's on-field wizardry knew no bounds. Here he hands the ball off as he is tackled in a Wallabies tour game in England in 1981.

Birthdate:	5 June 1959
Place of birth:	Sydney, New South Wales
Nickname:	Mullet
Caps:	25 (Wallaby #616)

A fly-half of sheer genius, Mark Ella had a brief but spectacular Test career featuring three famous wins over the All Blacks and a personal grand slam of Test tries on the all-conquering Wallaby tour of Britain and Ireland in 1984. Along with his brothers Glen and Gary, Mark revolutionised attacking rugby in Australia. The trio initially captured global attention on the unbeaten Australian Schools European tour in 1977–78 utilising their flat-line, close formation, ball-in-hand strategy. But Mark soon became the lead man as he displayed his scintillating handling and instinctive running lines. According to David Campese, 'He is the best player I have known or seen.'

Mark Ella stunned the rugby world when he called time on his short but brilliant career at just 25 years of age. His premature loss to the code was a major blow given his performance level had just climbed to dazzling heights. From the outskirts of La Perouse to the great rugby cathedrals of Britain, Mark made an indelible impression. His soft hands, and often-mesmerising running lines helped transform the Wallaby backline into a lethal attacking force. By 1984 they were simply unstoppable. His love for the game was reflected in his schoolboy approach: keep the ball in hand, keep it alive and have fun in the process. In concert with brothers

Brothers Glen, Gary and Mark Ella captivated the rugby public in the late 1970s and early 1980s with their skills and sense of fun.

Glen and Gary, kicking was a last resort. Their aim was to create time and space and they did so in a revolutionary manner employing rapid ball movement from close formation in a flat alignment to feed a constant wave of support runners operating from different angles.

Mark's mother May and father Gordon raised their 12 children in a shanty dwelling. Living conditions were primitive. There was no hot running water and the toilet was an outhouse. As youngsters the three rugby brothers slept on a mattress in their parents' bedroom. The remaining nine kids slept in the other two bedrooms. A daily activity for the boys was to collect wood for the fuel stove. Gordon was the breadwinner and worked at the nearby oil refinery. May was the quintessential matriarch and a strict disciplinarian. 'Mum taught us to treat everybody as equals,' Mark recalled in his biography *ELLA* co-authored with Bret Harris. 'We grew up in a big Aboriginal community and she just wanted us to fit in with every nationality. She wanted us to do well, but to do well you had to do well at school. You had to respect people. You had to fit in.'

Despite the financial hardship, family life in the Ella household

'As youngsters the three rugby brothers slept on a mattress in their parents' bedroom. The remaining nine kids slept in the other two bedrooms.'

was rewarding. In summer the brothers were never short of leisure activities – swimming, diving for coins and fishing, playing golf on their makeshift three-hole course or collecting balls at the local golf club. Growing up, their friends included future Wallaby Lloyd Walker, future coaching guru Eddie Jones and Australian Schoolboys teammate Darryl Lester who lived next door.

Mark and his brothers came to rugby prominence at Matraville High School under coach Geoff Mould who pinpointed Mark's silky skills. 'He had a latent ability to understand the requirements of fly-half. He underplayed his game to produce results. He ran straight and his soft pass allowed him to immediately support. I can honestly say I never saw Mark drop a ball.' One of the school's more noteworthy wins was against the wealthy Greater Public Schools powerhouse St Joseph's College in a pre-season trial at Latham Park, South Coogee. 'We turned up looking like a bunch of liquorice allsorts,' Mark recalled. 'They turned up with two busloads of supporters (in school uniform). These guys are in all their regalia. Boots are perfect. We had Souths socks, Matto socks, holes in our jerseys, fuzzy hair. It was a weird feeling.' Two interested spectators that day were future Wallaby coach Bob Dwyer and Wallaby legend Cyril Towers. Both men were destined to have a huge influence on Mark's career, Bob as his club and national coach and Cyril as a personal mentor. Matraville remained unbeaten in 24 games in 1977, the Ellas' final year, scoring an incredible 228 tries, 122 of those by the wingers.

Later that year Mould became head coach of the unbeaten national schoolboy team. That trailblazing squad rewrote the coaching manuals drawing large crowds on their celebrated 16-match sweep through the UK, Ireland, Holland and Japan. They scored 566 points for, to only 97 against. Although 10 members of that team went on to achieve Wallaby status (and Wally Lewis became a rugby league immortal), Mark and his two brothers were the

stars of the show. After the tour the three Ellas bypassed colts and were rushed straight into senior grade rugby at Randwick. Youngest brother Gary was first to debut in the top grade but when the trio was finally selected together, mayhem was the operative word for opposition defences. A 63-0 demolition of previously unbeaten Northern Suburbs emphatically confirmed the arrival of a new and exciting rugby phenomenon.

In 1979 Mark and his identical twin Glen were selected in the Australian team for the Hong Kong Sevens. It was Mark's first taste of senior representative rugby and the new-look Aussie team wowed the fans with exhilarating running and passing, downing Samoa 39-3 in the final. Mark enjoyed a further taste of international football on his return. After missing selection for the first interstate clash (Queensland won 48-10) Mark was chosen at fly-half in the Sydney team to meet Ireland. He seized the chance to oppose the mercurial Tony Ward. The result was Ireland's only loss on their tour Down Under. Mark's surprise 'in-your-face' attacking style helped prise open the rattled defence for two well-conceived tries. Selection in the Wallaby squad to

Mark Ella attempts to make his way past All Blacks defence during a Bledisloe Cup match in 1982.

Ella scores Australia's final try in the win over Wales at Cardiff Arms Park during the Wallabies' famed grand slam tour of Britain and Ireland in 1984.

tour Argentina followed but there was no Test spot for the 20-year-old with Paul McLean and Tony Melrose ahead in the pecking order.

Ella's big moment finally arrived the following year despite initially being overlooked at fly-half in favour of Michael Hawker in the one-off Test in Suva against Fiji. (Melrose had gone to rugby league.) An eye-catching performance for Sydney in their 13-13 draw against the All Blacks convinced national coach Bob Templeton that Mark was ready, especially as McLean was unavailable with a knee injury. When Mark told his mother May he'd been selected at fly-half to

face New Zealand at the SCG, she fainted. Andrew Slack had been chosen at inside-centre but when he succumbed to a shoulder injury, former schoolboy stars Hawker and Michael O'Connor were united in the centres. Templeton changed tack and told the three youngsters to work out how they wanted to play.

'To his credit he (Templeton) gave us our freedom,' Mark reflected in *ELLA*. 'We said there is only one way we know how to play. Let's have a go and run them around. And that's what we did.' Mark's confidence level skyrocketed before the game. 'That was the best combination I played in with the Wallabies. Apart from being very talented individually, it was the way we combined together. We complemented each other. I was a good distributor and support player, Hawker was solid and ran hard and straight and O'Connor was a freak who could do anything.' Feeding off a solid forward platform led by Tony Shaw and including impressive rookies Simon Poidevin and Steve Williams, the Aussie backs ran riot. Mark was the spearhead and the Wallabies clinched the series and the Bledisloe Cup with a breathtaking 26-10 win in the Third Test at the SCG. It was Australia's first three-Test series win against New Zealand on home soil since 1934 and the largest-ever winning margin against the All Blacks.

The three Ella brothers were then chosen for the 1981–82 tour of Britain and Ireland. Beforehand, team manager Sir Nicholas Shehadie organised a fundraiser at the City Tattersalls Club so that May and Gordon could join the Test match portion of the tour. The return of the now famous brothers was headlined in the English media and the Wallabies were hailed as world-beaters. Alas, the Wallabies never matched the hype. The trio failed to establish full fluency when selected together. Mark was personally below

his best as he tried to improve his kicking game and adapt to a more conservative team pattern which required him to stand deeper.

Not selected, Ella watched from the grandstand as Australia downed Ireland 16-12 but then fell away when in winning positions against Wales, Scotland and England. In Cardiff he stagnated on the reserves bench as the Wallabies butchered their chance of a Grand Slam with the loss to Wales. He was finally recalled for the Scottish Test with Paul McLean shifting to inside-centre. Australia scored three tries to one but kicked only one goal from seven attempts. In the Test match at Twickenham, goal kicking was again the team's Achilles heel. England was outscored by two tries to one but the Wallabies only managed one goal from five attempts. Mark revealed his frustrations. 'The other teams [Wales, Scotland and England] were inferior to Ireland and we lost to all of those teams. That sums up the tour. We wasted the other three Test matches.' Thankfully, Mark and many of the same teammates would return to Britain two years later to comprehensively rewrite history.

Randwick coach Bob Dwyer had made Mark first grade captain in

1980 and it proved a springboard for three straight premiership victories. On the back of that momentum Dwyer was appointed national coach in 1982, replacing Templeton. He immediately went 'all-in'. Dwyer controversially chose Mark and Glen over Queensland heroes Paul McLean and Roger Gould for the First Test against Scotland at Ballymore. A barrage of criticism ensued in the local media and by game day Mark and Glen were walking on eggshells, rattled by the torrent of negative attention. When sections of the crowd booed as the Wallabies took the field, Australian rugby hit its lowest ebb.

In his biography, Mark summed up his despair. 'It was terrible. They booed the Wallabies. I felt like crap. The boos were directed at Glen and me. Disgraceful.' The brothers both had forgettable games as the Aussies bombed at least four tries allowing Scotland to score an upset 12-7 victory. McLean and Gould were reinstated for the Second Test at the SCG and both had superb games in the record 33-9 triumph. Paul kicked eight goals from nine attempts and Roger scored two tries from fullback – then a record against any 'tier one' country.

But emerging from the aftermath of the Ballymore disaster came Mark's greatest honour. When nine Queenslanders, including the three most recent Test captains (Mark Loane, Tony Shaw and McLean) withdrew from the Wallaby tour of New Zealand, Dwyer offered Mark the captaincy. After initially rejecting the idea, Ella saw his coach's reasoning. 'Bob needed support. He was under siege. He needed somebody he could rely on. Whether I was the best person for captain is debatable, but Bob needed friends and I was one of his biggest supporters. I guess that's why I got the nod.' Twelve new Wallabies were named in the touring squad including an exciting teenager, David Campese.

The three Ella brothers never played a Test together but came closest in the First Test against the Kiwis in Christchurch. Roger Gould passed a last minute fitness test which denied Glen the opportunity to join Mark and Gary in the starting team. The All Blacks won the series 2-1 but only after overcoming a half-time deficit in the Auckland decider. Australia's highlight was the stunning Second Test victory in Wellington. Crucially, Mark won the toss in that game and ran with the first half gale to build a 19-3 lead at

Mark Ella succeeded Trevor Allan as the ABC's television rugby expert in 1987.

the break thanks to two spectacular tries. The second half saw one of the great Wallaby defensive efforts with back-rowers Poidevin, Peter Lucas and Chris Roche ferociously chopping down every All Black who came their way. Soon after, Mark's leadership and ability were duly recognised when he was named Young Australian of the Year.

After a lacklustre tour of France in 1983 Dwyer was out as Wallaby coach and premiership winning Manly coach Alan Jones was in. Ella lost the captaincy to Andrew Slack and, unbeknown to most, his departure from international rugby later that season had already been decided. Four years earlier, Mark had told his girlfriend Kim that he would retire when he turned 25 and marry her. Being stripped of the captaincy only reinforced his conviction there was no turning back. Wife Kim believes the setback was a blessing. 'It took the pressure off him. Andrew [Slack] let him run his own race over there. The Grand Slam was a gift. It wasn't something he aspired to. It just came to him.'

It sure did! Mark's spectacular 'loop' try against England at Twickenham set up a record 19-3 victory. The run-around move was considered obstruction in Britain but Mark called the ploy just once on the whole tour, realising a New Zealand referee was in charge that day. Against Ireland Australia was in trouble trailing 9-3 midway through the second half. But two Ella drop goals with either foot steadied the ship before he engineered and scored the winning try after handling twice in the movement. The Wales Test was all about the mighty Wallaby forward pack but Mark had the final

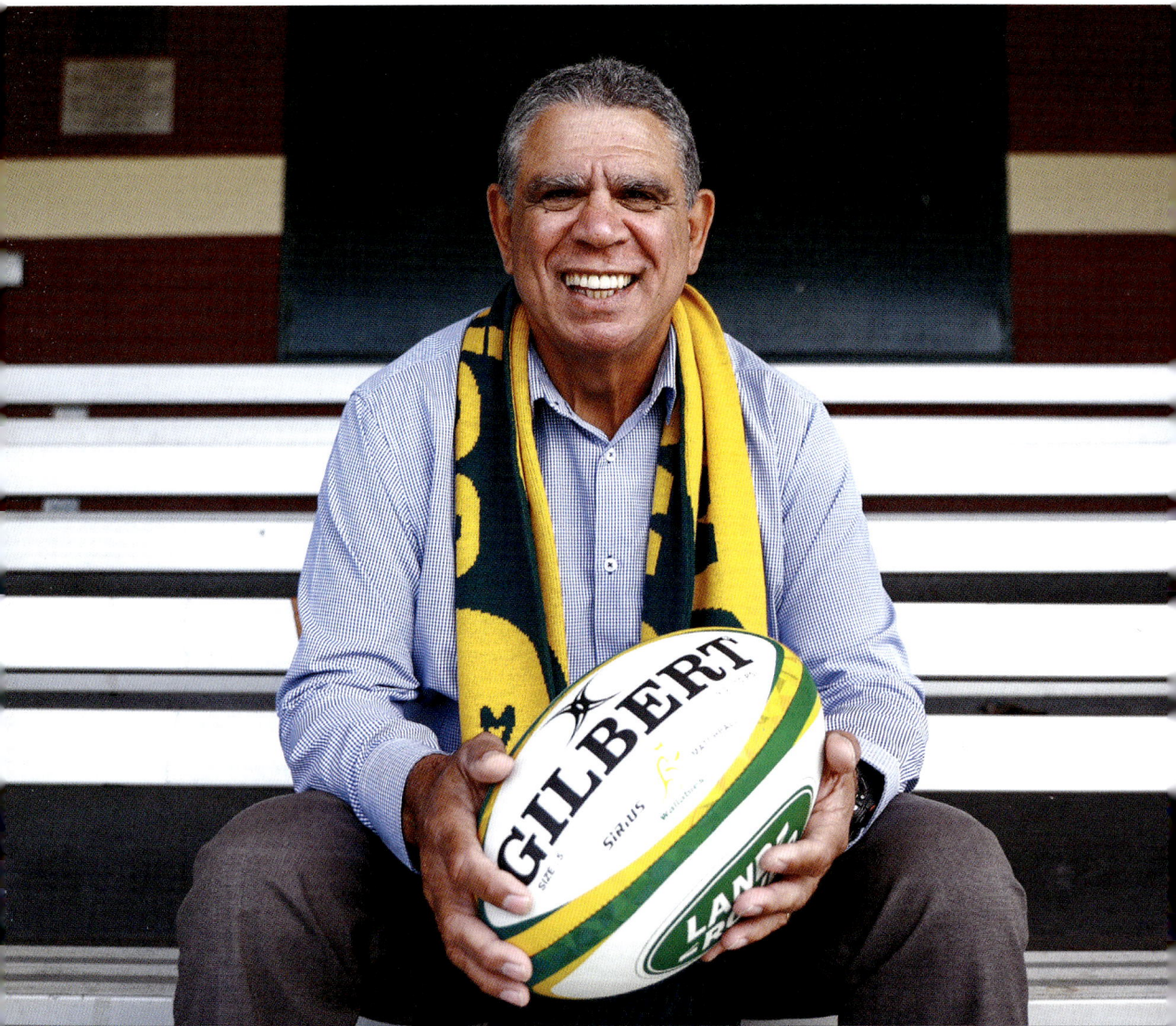

'The best player I have known or seen,' is David Campese's take on Mark Ella.

say with a clever intercept try after anticipating that their opponent's pass would come his way.

The Scots met a similar fate at the hands of the Wallabies, but Mark can thank roommate Roger Gould for the try that completed his personal grand slam. Again he handled twice as Roger turned the ball back inside when the defence thought it was going out to Campese. Ella remembers his elation: 'I always say for a guy who was slow and couldn't sidestep, to score four tries in four Tests was pretty special. I had played in 21 Test matches and scored two tries. Now I'd scored four in a row. I knew I was going to retire.' Ousted coach Dwyer was gushing in his praise. 'Jones' decision to let Mark call the shots was a masterstroke. He played fantastically well. Mark was just a genius. He carried that tour.'

Mark was the first Indigenous Australian to captain Australia in any sport. Inducted into the International Rugby Hall of Fame in 1997, he now lives on the NSW Central Coast with wife Kim. They have two children, a son Simon and daughter Nicole who is a lawyer. His journey after the Wallabies has been varied and fascinating. From TV commentator with ABC Sport to weekly columnist with *The Australian* newspaper, to marketer, businessman and successful rugby coach in Italy, Mark Ella has always kept active. Outside rugby, one of his greatest regrets is that he didn't get to see his sister Marcia play in more than one of her 18 international appearances for the Australian Diamonds Netball team.

During his playing career Ella received many lucrative offers to switch to rugby league but always resisted. In 1985 the St George Dragons offered him 'telephone numbers'. They needed a five-eighth and Michael O'Connor was desperate to reunite with his good mate. Mark rang 'The King' – Wally Lewis – in Brisbane for a second opinion. (Lewis still rates Mark the best footballer he played with in either code.) When told the amount on offer, Wally replied, 'Shit, that's more than I'm getting!' Say no more.

7

DAVID CAMPESE

Birthdate:	21 October 1962
Place of birth:	Queanbeyan, New South Wales
Nickname:	Campo
Caps:	101 (Wallaby #623)

He was rugby's quintessential showstopper. Campese made his Test debut at 19 against New Zealand in Christchurch in 1982, the first of 29 Internationals against the All Blacks over the next 14 years. He was a member of the 1984 'Grand Slam' Wallabies tour of the UK and Ireland and the triumphant 1986 Bledisloe Cup team. In the 1991 Rugby World Cup he was undisputed Player of the Tournament and a year later scored his 50th Test try in Cape Town against South Africa. Campese played his 100th Test in Padova against Italy in 1996.

David Campese, during his 15 season career in Wallaby colours, was an unabashed 'freedom fighter' for attacking rugby. His first instinct was to identify space and run, then decide whether he, or a teammate, was best placed to continue. He was never intimidated by an opponent.

'Campo' (as he is still universally known) was always prepared to take a chance and try something different. That unorthodoxy stemmed from a firm belief in his own abilities. He knew he could do things that other players could not, and relished being the player who produced the unpredictable. His unique talent for improvisation delighted rugby connoisseurs the world over.

The second eldest of four siblings born to Gianantonio and Joan Campese, David's co-ordination and athletic ability were soon evident. He played junior rugby league

Campese scored one of the great solo tries of the 1991 Rugby World Cup when he got around John Kirwan and a host of New Zealand defenders in the semi-final.

for the Queanbeyan Blues for eight seasons until he was 16. (By that stage he was actually a better golfer than footballer, having won the ACT-Monaro Schoolboy Golf Championship as a 15-year-old.)

But rugby union was destined to be where his brilliant future lay. After a verbal lashing on some defensive lapses from his junior league coach, rival rugby club Queanbeyan Whites snared Campese as a prized recruit. His impact was immediate and the local newspapers began calling him 'Dashing David'. In 1982 he was selected for the Australian Under

21 team to play the curtain raiser at the Sydney Test. Campo's dazzling attack from fullback carved up his New Zealand counterparts and was the main talking point that evening, despite the senior team's record win over Scotland. Wallaby honours seemed sure to follow swiftly.

When nine members of the Queensland team made themselves unavailable for the three-Test tour of New Zealand, new national coach Bob Dwyer grabbed the opportunity to select the budding superstar. On arrival in New Zealand, Campese was asked in a press conference about his upcoming clash with the great Kiwi winger Stu Wilson. His 'Stu who?' response was taken out of context by the local media who saw it as a brash insult. Not so. David later revealed that growing up in Queanbeyan, he'd followed league and had never heard of 'Super Stu'.

On tour, the teenage sensation literally hit the ground running and developed an instant, almost telepathic rapport with newly appointed skipper, Mark Ella. After the 26-10 win over Manawatu, authors Chester and McMillan reported in *The Visitors,* 'In Mark Ella and 19-year-old Campese the Wallabies had two outstanding players who exhibited a confidence that approached arrogance.' Campese was even sometimes referred to as the 'fourth Ella'.

Dwyer later revealed that he'd been in two minds about picking Campo for the First Test. That was until he was approached by several of the senior players who brought an explicit message: 'Coach, you've got to pick the kid.' Campo was one of a remarkable six new caps: centre Gary Ella, No. 8 Peter Lucas and the entire front row of John Coolican, Bruce Malouf and Andy McIntyre. An injury cloud over fullback Roger Gould had Glen Ella on standby. But Gould proved his fitness and history

was denied a unique footnote as the three Ella brothers were never selected together for a Test match.

As predicted, legendary All Black winger Stu Wilson went head-to-head with Campese and later admitted that he'd been outplayed by the precocious teenager. In *Ironbark Legends – David Campese* by David Clark, Wilson revealed: 'It was his "vision" that made him stand out. Add to that his slick ball skills, the ability to step off either foot, his acceleration and his anticipation and you had a player of rare class. I know we were always concerned that whenever he got the ball something was always on and he had to be watched. "What the hell is he going to do now?" was the frantic question in the All Black backline that showed our obsession with him.'

A crowd of 38,000 saw the understrength Wallabies lose 23-16 in Christchurch. Campo had the final say when he fielded a cross-field kick

'On tour, the teenage sensation literally hit the ground running and developed an instant, almost telepathic rapport with newly appointed skipper, Mark Ella.'

from skipper Ella and then left the world's best winger in his wake.

Australia made two changes for the Second Test in Wellington, both in the front row. Experienced John Meadows was joined by powerful hooker Lance Walker. Ella won the toss and elected to run with a big southerly wind and the visitors made the most of their good fortune. Campese handled twice in a stunning attack before side-stepping All Black skipper Graham Mourie to send Gary Ella over. Then right on half-time a sweeping Wallaby attack saw more than half the side handle before sending Campo across beside the upright for the try of the tour – a score that certainly ranks with the most stirring tries in Test match history.

It was a knockout blow and gave the Australians a match-winning 19-3 lead. For any remaining doubters, those tries in each of his first two Tests against the All Blacks were testimony to the arrival of Campese as an international rugby star.

But the home team prevailed two weeks later in Auckland to regain the Bledisloe Cup. Their forward pack gained the upper hand in the last quarter to win 33-18 after the Wallabies had led 15-12 at half-

time. For young Campese, this campaign was an unforgettable start to his illustrious career. Bob Dwyer's Wallabies thrilled New Zealand with their attacking rugby, winning 10 of 14 matches. *DB Rugby Annual* editor, Bob Howitt, even named Campo alongside Robbie Deans, Andy Haden, Allan Hewson and Murray Mexted as one of five Players of the Year.

Wallaby fans were treated to a Campese try fest the following year against the USA at the SCG. In a debut Test on home soil, his four tries equalled Greg Cornelsen's incredible record haul against the All Blacks at Eden Park in 1978. But a series loss to France in 1983 signalled the end of Bob Dwyer's first stint as Australian coach. Alan Jones filled the breach and made an immediate impact. By year's end the Wallabies had swept aside the four Home Unions in Britain and Ireland to record their historic grand slam. Jones introduced two exciting newcomers at the start of the campaign and both excelled. Scrum-half Nick Farr-Jones struck up a compelling partnership with Mark Ella while No. 8 Steve Tuynman proved a massive asset in the lineout and as a ball runner.

Fourteen years after his Test debut Campo still posed a menacing threat against Wales at the Sydney Football Stadium in 1996.

Campese was still a prolific try scorer in 1993, more than a decade into his international career.

Campese scored two tries in the Slam clincher against Scotland in Edinburgh. Relieved of the captaincy in favour of Andrew Slack, Ella scored a personal grand slam of tries and promptly announced his premature retirement at just 25. The euphoria of Australia's triumph papered over the realisation that the spine-tingling and often magical on-field chemistry of kindred spirits Campo and Ella would be seen no more in a Wallaby Test jumper.

A highwire trapeze artist by nature, David Campese was always vulnerable to a rough landing. In 1986, after winning the First Test in Wellington, the Wallabies were robbed of a series victory in the Second Test when Welsh referee Derek Bevan disallowed a legitimate try by Tuynman. Coach Alan Jones had been Campo's greatest admirer but after a wretched day at fullback, the relationship temporarily soured. Later that night in Jones' room, David endured a withering tongue-lashing from the coach for his inept performance.

Campese was so distraught in a nightclub a few hours later that he declared he was ready to retire from rugby. It was distressing that such a gifted athlete and entertainer could become so despondent and agitated. The world's rugby enthusiasts can be grateful that Nick Farr-Jones and then later commentator Mark Ella consoled Campo that night, and redemption came swiftly. After switching back to wing, Campese scored the Bledisloe Cup-clinching try at Eden Park. Superbly led by Andrew Slack, Jones' Wallabies became the first Australian team to win a three-Test series on New Zealand soil.

'This platform provided Campo with the opportunity to showcase his full repertoire, from the trademark "goose-step" and rapier acceleration to his high speed change-of-direction and deception. The World Cup was the perfect time to break the shackles and he didn't disappoint.'

David played his rugby on the highwire – without a safety net – and sometimes there was a price to pay for this risk-prone mindset. The one incident that will always be remembered came in the closing stages of the deciding Test against the British Lions in 1989 at the Sydney Football Stadium. After trying to run the ball out from his goal line, his errant pass to fullback Greg Martin effectively cost Australia the series. That incident was the low point of an otherwise glittering career but such moments were few and, in overall context, insignificant. 'You have to try and try again and you have to fail' is his response. 'That's how you become a winner. Winners take chances, like everybody else they fear failing. If you don't make mistakes you don't learn.'

Campo hammered home that point at the 1991 Rugby World Cup. After being reinstated as Wallaby coach in 1988, Bob Dwyer developed a team studded with world-class players. Alongside Campo he fielded new skipper Farr-Jones, Michael Lynagh and Tim Horan. It was a backline arsenal ready to blitz all comers. Dwyer also had a powerful, well-balanced forward pack which included exciting young giant John Eales in the second row and the experienced back-row gladiator Simon Poidevin.

This platform provided Campo with the opportunity to showcase his full repertoire, from the trademark 'goose-step' and rapier acceleration to his high speed change-of-direction and deception. The World Cup was the perfect time to break the shackles and he didn't disappoint. Campese skinned Argentina in Llanelli and Wales in Cardiff, broke Irish hearts in Dublin and then devastated the All Blacks a week later at the same venue. His diagonal run to score in the corner hoodwinked

the spooked Kiwi defence. Then came the miracle 'blind' over-the-shoulder pass to Horan just before the break, later adjudged 'Try of the Tournament'. 'Did you see that pass?' exclaimed the excited Australian TV commentator. 'The man is an absolute genius!' In those moments, Campese had given a true masterclass.

Aged 29, and now at the peak of his powers, Campo fulfilled his rugby destiny a week later when Australia downed England in an epic final. In that dizzy, euphoric moment he was not only a member of the best team in the world but as Player of the Tournament, he was effectively adjudged the best player in the world.

Although he played Test rugby for a further five years, Campo only rarely approached the peak of his World Cup glory days. In 1992 he scored his 50th Test try in Cape Town against the Springboks, the first 'post-apartheid' Test match since the two countries had last met in 1971. Then, as the son of an Italian immigrant winemaker, it was appropriate that coach Greg Smith afforded him the opportunity to play his 100th Test against Italy in Padova on the 1996 spring tour. Campese became the first

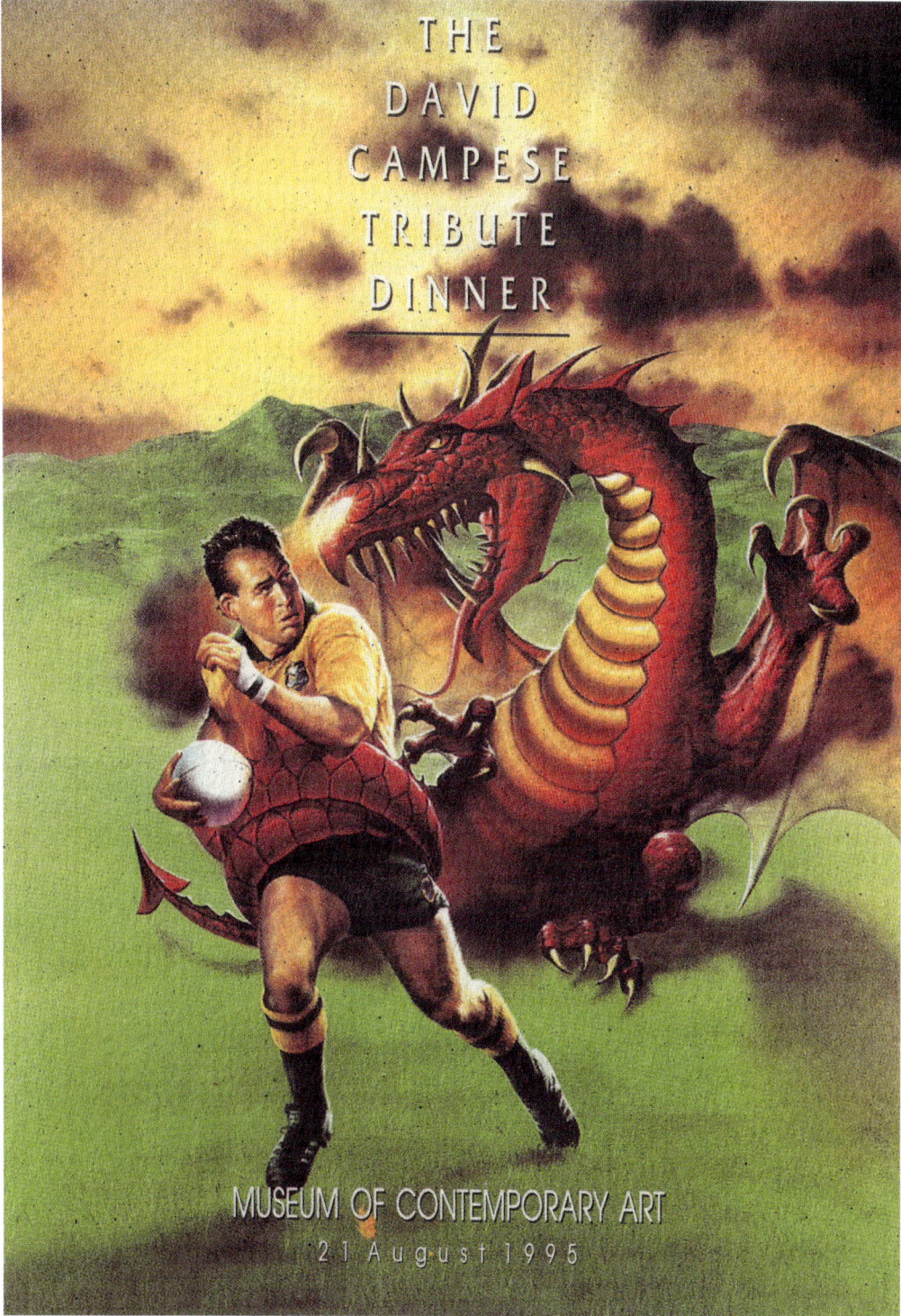

The David Campese Tribute Dinner menu booklet from 1995 featured somewhat abstract if appropriate cover artwork.

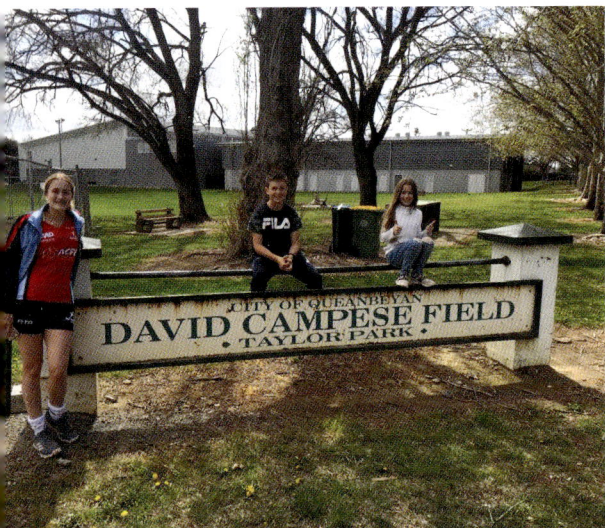

The three Campese siblings Sienna, Jason and Mercedes visit their dad's proud legacy in his hometown.

Wallaby to reach a century of caps and only the second player in the world after Frenchman Philippe Sella (111 Tests).

There was no fairytale try in Australia's 40-18 victory that day, but he was afforded a special honour by captain John Eales to make a solo entry onto the Campo-Plebiscito Sportivo to a standing ovation. In fact, Italy had been a second home for Campese. He'd played 10 seasons, based in Petrarca from 1984 to 1988 and then Amatori Milano from 1988 to 1993. In Milan he reconnected with his great mate Mark Ella who was the club coach. Campo loved the lifestyle and the accompanying 'sponsorship' benefits in what was ostensibly still an amateur era.

Campo's farewell at Cardiff Arms Park in 1996 capped a 12 match unbeaten tour for Greg Smith's Wallabies. They scored 453 points to 212 against and his veteran winger was the leading try scorer. There was then one last appearance in national colours at the Commonwealth Games in 1998 at Kuala Lumpur. At 35 he was still good enough to reproduce his maestro 'sevens' skills, helping Australia to a bronze medal.

David Campese was unquestionably one of a kind. So extravagantly gifted yet so vulnerable. He gave the impression that he was an easy target – a ready-made scapegoat for coaches when things went wrong. But that was the nature of his personal and sporting philosophy – sometimes dazzling, sometimes perplexing, and sometimes both of those qualities in the same breath. Here was a sportsman who translated rare ability into pleasure and fun for himself and the audience.

As an elite rugby player, Campo was a perfectionist. He became frustrated when he failed to reach his self-imposed high standards on the field. But Bob Dwyer believes that was also his great strength because he was willing to risk

'He gave the impression that he was an easy target – a readymade scapegoat for coaches when things went wrong. But that was the nature of his personal and sporting philosophy – sometimes dazzling, sometimes perplexing, and sometimes both of those qualities in the same breath.'

personal failure on the global stage in order to succeed. The indisputable truth is that he has always remained loyal to the game he loves so passionately.

In his evocative tome *Campese: The Last of the Dream Sellers*, James Curran warrants the final say. The modern history professor takes our hero out of his glass cage and explores his creative genius. 'Campese seemed to operate on cross-grained pure instinct: one that left many a defender not only clutching in vain at the invisible, but stranded in his audacity's slipstream. He followed no straight path, observed no rule book. Conjuring wizardry across the open field, his play was unbridled, unstructured, untamed,

unpredictable and, at times, uncontrollable. The result was some of the most exhilarating feats ever seen by an Australian sportsman.'

Campo finished his Test career with 101 Wallaby caps, 315 points and a world record 64 tries. To select the highest peak in his career is challenging but that first 40 minutes against the All Blacks in the 1991 World Cup semi-final is hard to ignore. Writing next day in the *Independent*, Irish great Tony Ward suggested: 'He's the Maradona, the Pele of international rugby all rolled into one. You can't put a value on his importance to the game. He's a breath of fresh air and I think perhaps the greatest player of all time. Without being too soppy, it was an honour to be at Lansdowne Road just to see him perform.'

International rugby will never again see the likes of David Campese. Forget his faults: here is a rugby man of true distinction – a Ferrari engine in a Rolls-Royce body. He inspired youngsters of his generation to always carry the sword to the opposition with excitement and flair. Every team needs a rebel of his ilk, someone brave enough to say, 'Let's give it a go, and bugger the consequences.' Thanks Campo.

Vice-captain Michael Lynagh was instrumental in the Wallabies' 1991 World Cup triumph.

8

MICHAEL LYNAGH

Birthdate:	25 October 1963
Place of birth:	Brisbane, Queensland
Nickname:	Noddy
Caps:	72 (Wallaby #642)

A supreme backline commander and champion goalkicker, he was one of Australian rugby's most gifted offspring. Michael Lynagh was a key architect in the Wallabies' stunning 1984 Grand Slam win, the 1986 Bledisloe triumph in New Zealand and the 1991 World Cup victory. His career was accelerated at every stage of development. He made the St Joseph's Gregory Terrace First XV at 15, debuted in first grade for University of Queensland at 18 and three weeks later was named in the Queensland senior team. His calm leadership and an ability to consistently deliver under the most intense pressure were the hallmarks of his game.

It will surprise many to learn that Michael Lynagh's first love as a youngster was cricket. Throughout his school years any serious rugby aspirations were in the 'afterthought' category. Football was something to do between cricket seasons. He made the St Joseph's College, Gregory Terrace First XI at 14 as a wicketkeeper/batsman, but his rugby talent was unmistakable

and ultimately the choice between rugby and cricket would be made for him.

Michael's early sporting pursuits were centred on the Queensland Gold Coast where he successfully tried soccer and rugby league. From under six to under eight, he played for the Musgrave Hill Rockets soccer team demonstrating exceptional ability at centre half and earning selection in successive Gold Coast representative teams. In Fifth Grade he was also a dynamic force in the Aquinas College four-stone-seven rugby league team where he impressed as a skilful lock and second row.

The four-strong Lynagh family consisting of dad Ian, mum Marie and sister Jane moved back to Brisbane in 1974 where Michael commenced the first of his eight years at Gregory Terrace. The new headmaster, Brother Barry Buckley, had a profound effect on the shape of his student's future as a sportsman and person. At the first school assembly, the head had a simple message: 'You'll only get out of this school what you put into it.' As the young Lynagh later reflected in his biography *Michael Lynagh: The Authorized Biography* by Andrew Slack; 'That line has stayed with me to this day. Pretty simple stuff, but I decided to put it to the test and my life to date has been rewarded beyond my wildest dreams.'

In 1978, Michael's father uprooted the family to study for his doctorate in psychology at Oregon State University. That presented Michael with a fourth football code exposure. He was selected in the Crescent Valley High gridiron team on the strength of his prodigious punt kicking. He happily admits that the combative nature of American football definitely highlighted the prerequisites of toughness and resilience for his future rugby exploits.

Michael returned to Brisbane with his mother and sister for the start of the 1979 school year at Gregory Terrace. There he came under the watch of outstanding First XV coach Lester Hampson who won five GPS premierships in six years. Years later Lester revealed he'd had no hesitation elevating his talented 15-year-old straight into the senior school team at fly-half. 'From the first time I saw him I knew he was something special. The thing I remember is that he had the softest hands. Often a halfback might fire a bullet pass out to a fly-half and you'd hear the slap as the hands met the ball. You'd hear nothing when Lynagh caught it. His ball-handling skills were superb – he really stood out. The potential was there for anyone to see.' Three years in the First XV led to selection in Queensland under-age teams, the Australian Under 17 side and ultimately the Australian Schoolboys

Lynagh played his first game for Queensland in 1981 as a raw 18-year-old against Wairarapa Bush.

team for their 1981-82 unbeaten tour of the UK and Ireland.

After eight glorious years at Gregory Terrace, where he'd captained both the First XV and First XI, Michael returned from that schoolboy tour to face the big wide world. As local rugby clubs clamoured for his presence and discussions took place with senior rugby identities, he came to the realization that his cricket aspirations had been hit for six, in effect demolished by his higher-profiled rugby successes. So rapid was his ascent in his first year out of school that when nine Queenslanders withdrew from the Wallaby tour of New Zealand, coach Bob Dwyer wanted Michael in the squad. But fellow selector and Queensland coach, the late Bob Templeton, had the final say as he

later explained. 'He was obviously a very talented young kid and we could break his heart by sending him on what looked like being a very arduous tour. I felt very strongly about it. Both Dwyer and John Bain, the chairman of selectors, thought he should go, but I was insistent that they were trying to rush him too much. We could have taken him but we'd have been running the risk of destroying his confidence.'

Although selected as a Wallaby tourist to France and Italy in 1983, 20-year-old Lynagh remained firmly in the shadow of national skipper Mark Ella. But his eagerly anticipated Test debut was just around the corner. The big moment arrived in June the following year when he was chosen at inside-centre against Fiji in Suva. Australia won 16-3 and Michael kicked three

In the thick of the action against Canterbury at Ballymore in 1987. Lynagh started 17 Tests with Wallaby skipper Andrew Slack, seen here in support.

penalties in deplorable rain-sodden conditions. But it was missed goal kicks by David Campese and Ella during the ensuing series against the All Blacks that proved a game changer. Although dropped after his debut in Fiji, Lynagh returned as inside-centre and principal goalkicker on the Grand Slam tour of Britain. It was a tough call to replace established incumbent Michael Hawker, but the right one. Coach Jones wanted a long-term goalkicker and Michael was already the best in the country. Unbeknown to teammates, Ella had confided in Lynagh the previous year that he would retire after the '84 tour and the Wallaby No. 10 jumper would then be his. Mark was good to his word and the rugby world was stunned when he announced his retirement at just 25 after clinching his personal grand slam of tries in the Test against Scotland. Lynagh was the top pointscorer on tour with 98 and scored 42 in the Tests. Ella stepped down knowing he had a readymade and highly talented replacement.

'Michael Lynagh became a trailblazer over the next 11 seasons. He chalked up a world record total of 911 points in his 72 Tests'

Michael Lynagh became a trailblazer over the next 11 seasons. He chalked up a world record total of 911 points in his 72 Tests including the most goals and most penalty goals. His Test match half-back partnership with Nick Farr-Jones endured for nine seasons and also established a new world record. Additionally, he scored 1,166 points for Queensland in 100 appearances. In *Born to Lead* author and Wallaby Max Howell made this glowing evaluation: 'He could sidestep, swerve, use change of pace, "read" a game and control a match, and he could lift the morale of a team as he kept kicking points between the uprights. He was safe on defence, his hands were impeccable and he had guts. Michael Lynagh was one of the greatest players to wear the green and gold, a multi-talented athlete of rare dimensions.'

The historic 1984 Grand Slam sweep of Britain and Ireland re-established Australia in rugby's

upper echelons but only a series win over the All Blacks would affirm any claims to number one spot in the global hierarchy. That opportunity arrived two years later on New Zealand soil. The incident-packed series against the Kiwis went down to the wire after Australia won the First Test in Wellington by 13-12 and then the Kiwis, boosted by their returning Cavalier tourists to South Africa, won the second game in Dunedin by the same score. Played before 48,000 fans, the decider in Auckland was a titanic struggle as the tourists repelled a ferocious first half onslaught before pulling away in the second term. Lynagh's sure goalkicking was instrumental. A conversion and four penalties sealed the Wallabies' first (and only) three-Test series win in New Zealand. But there was no repeat performance at the inaugural Rugby World Cup the following year. French fullback Serge Blanco scored a searing last ditch try to torpedo Australia in the semi-final at Sydney's Concord Oval. That loss remains the biggest disappointment of Michael's career.

Australia's shot at World Cup redemption arrived four years later in Britain and Ireland. Under new coach Bob Dwyer the

Aussies were in rampant form with Campese the star of the show. But in the three big finals that counted 'Noddy' was central to the Wallaby strategy. He executed a magical chip kick for Campo's try of the tournament against the All Blacks, then sat calmly in the driver's seat against England in the final. His two penalties and a conversion were crucial components in the winning 12-6 score. He scored 66 of Australia's 126 points during the Cup and was one of the six Wallabies to play all six games. He was a unanimous choice for the World Cup XV after the tournament.

If there was one defining moment in Michael Lynagh's illustrious Wallaby career it most assuredly was his match-winning try in the quarter-final against Ireland in Dublin. Trailing 18-15 with just four minutes left, and facing the prospect of an inglorious exit from the tournament, the stand-in captain stepped up to the plate and gave his desperate teammates an escape route. Clarity and positivity were the key. There was still time to get the ball up the other end and then hold it at all costs. The backs, he proclaimed, would do the rest. No truer words have been spoken by any Wallaby

captain under siege. They were revealed in his biography: 'Be calm and controlled. There's still plenty of time left (four minutes). From the kick-off we will kick the ball long and to the left. The forwards must secure clean possession and we'll go from there. If ever in doubt what to do with the ball, just hold it tightly and head towards their line. We *will win* this game.'

Winger Rob Egerton pressured the deep kick-off that eventually led to an attacking scrum. Michael dismissed the option of a drop goal, electing instead to go for the try. From the ensuing set move he fired a cut-out pass to fullback Marty Roebuck who created space for his outside men. David Campese was tackled just short and then desperately fed the ball backwards. At that moment, Michael employing his schoolboy wicket-keeping skills, scooped up the 'make or break' half volley to score beside the corner post. In *Michael Lynagh* author Andrew Slack succinctly articulated the significance of our hero's composure and precision finish. 'He plunged through a desperate but ineffective tackle by Irish winger Jack Clarke and scored the most crucial try in the history of Australian rugby – a four-point *coup*

Raising the 1991 World Cup trophy with Simon Poidevin.

de grâce that crushed Irish hopes and turned Nick Farr-Jones' Wallabies from also-rans to world champions.'

1992 was a monumental year for Australian rugby. The code enjoyed unprecedented popularity, especially after the world champions downed the All Blacks to regain the Bledisloe Cup on home soil. But there was still one more issue to settle following South Africa's re-entry on the world rugby stage. A one-off Test against the Springboks was scheduled for Cape Town and, after losing to New Zealand the previous week in Johannesburg, the home forward pack was outgunned on a soggy Newlands pitch. The majority of Australia's starting World Cup side took the field. Campese scored his

50th Test try and Michael slotted three penalties and a conversion in the emphatic 26-3 victory. His amazing 47-Test partnership with Farr-Jones finished on a high. For the first time in history, after beating every possible challenger, the Wallabies could rightly claim to be undisputed champions of the world.

After the 1991 World Cup Lynagh was given special dispensation to join leading Italian club Benetton and was employed by the fashion-ware company. The arrangement allowed him to still fulfil Wallaby commitments and, fortuitously, introduced him to his future wife Isabella, herself a former elite junior tennis player. National coach Dwyer appointed him captain to replace Farr-Jones and he led Australia to 10 wins in 13 Tests through to the quarter-final loss against England at the 1995 Rugby World Cup. Four weeks earlier he'd demonstrated his readiness for a third Cup campaign with a record Test match haul of 28 points against Argentina at Ballymore.

While the loss to England was a disappointing end to his international career the onset of professional rugby presented new opportunities. Michael joined the privately owned English club Saracens for the 1996–97 season. Glamour teammates included the world's most-capped player, Philippe

Lynagh paid close attention to mental preparation long before it was fashionable. It contributed greatly to his effectiveness as a goalkicker.

Sella, and South Africa's World Cup-winning skipper Francois Pienaar. Two seasons later, Noddy steered the club to a resounding win in the English club final downing Wasps by 48-18. At 34 and now in the twilight of his playing days, it was a glorious note to call time, 16 years after his Queensland debut as a raw 18-year-old against Wairarapa Bush. It was a prestige addition to his impressive collection of premiership-winning trophies with University of Queensland and Benetton.

Throughout his distinguished career Michael preferred to be a quiet achiever. His reserved nature underlined a thoughtful and sensitive approach to everything he tackled. Father Ian and mum Marie taught him to focus on process at a young age. Understanding the means to the end, he listened attentively, practised relentlessly and then backed himself. He completed a Bachelor of Human Movement at the University of Queensland where his professor was none other than Wallaby Max Howell, who'd watched his development as a player and person from close quarters. In *Born to Lead* Howell observed: 'He was a thoughtful individual who was his own man. He was never one for the grandiose gesture. But he was never a follower either. He was an unconventional team leader, though his style of "power sharing" is more in vogue nowadays. In most instances, he let his boot and play do the talking.'

His versatility meant he was equally effective in different positions. He played 64 Tests at No. 10, seven at centre and one at fullback with an overall win rate of 72%. Lynagh played in three World Cup tournaments for Australia, 1987 when they reached the semi-final, in 1991 when they were Champions, and in 1995 when they were quarter-finalists. He also owns the unique status of scoring points in each of his first 59 Tests and reached a double century in his 15th international.

Michael has enjoyed a successful business career which included the role of managing director of Dow Jones EMEA. He is also a respected TV pundit in the UK and his two sons are following in their father's rugby path. Louis is contracted to England and Tom plays for the Queensland Reds. Lynagh was inducted into the Sport Australia Hall of Fame in 1999 and the International Rugby Hall of Fame two years later. He is a Member of the Order of Australia.

Nick Farr-Jones captained the Wallabies during the triumphant 1991 World Cup campaign.

9

NICK FARR-JONES

Birthdate:	18 April 1962
Place of birth:	Sydney, New South Wales
Nickname:	Farr
Caps:	63 (Wallaby #645)

Nick Farr-Jones rates among our greatest Wallaby captains. A complete scrum-half with the robust physicality of a back-rower, his inspired leadership guided the Wallabies to Rugby World Cup glory at Twickenham in 1991. He possessed a fast, accurate pass on both sides and an uncanny instinct to break open defences on the blindside. Farr-Jones' intuitive ability to consistently take the best option made him indispensable. He formed a match-winning combination with Mark Ella on the 1984 Grand Slam Wallaby tour and then forged a brilliant inside-back partnership with Michael Lynagh spanning a world record 47 Test matches.

A survey of the Farr-Jones family tree reveals an impressive list of high sporting achievers, especially on his late mother Rosemary's side. She attended the select Kambala private girls school in Sydney and won the All Schools' 100 yards sprint and the 50 yards swimming championship. At Sydney University she was awarded sporting blues for swimming, athletics and basketball. Her lawyer father, Noel Burns, was also a champion schoolboy sprinter. Nick's late father Max, who operated the first night chemist in Sydney, was an excellent golfer and his brother Ross was an outstanding tennis player, winning the Combined High Schools Doubles Championship. Olympian John Cuneo was Max and Ross's cousin. He won the gold

Brothers Peter, Nick and Simon Farr-Jones.

medal in the Dragon class yachting event at the 1972 Munich Games.

Max and Rosemary harnessed this imposing sporting lineage for their three sons who were thrown into a wide array of sports. Young Nick's number one football code was soccer. Rugby wasn't even on the family's radar. At 10 years of age, he captained Lilli Pilli to win the state-wide Champion of Champions tournament. In *Nick Farr-Jones* by Peter FitzSimons, Nick's level of commitment was vividly recalled: 'His aim was not just to be a good soccer player, but to be the best.'

Father Max worked long hours in his pharmacy and, although rarely home for dinner, was always up early the next morning to take his three boys to swimming training at 5.30 am. Nick, in particular, hated that daily grind but always abided by his dad's wishes. The brothers were also introduced to the 'Nippers' at Eloura Beach Surf Club. Nick excelled at the beach flags event where the kids had to sprint from a standing start to grab one of a limited number of flags stuck in the sand. Speed off the mark, backed by a dose of raw aggression, proved to be an excellent grounding for later challenges on the great rugby grounds of the world. Max wanted his boys to be focused and disciplined in their sport. Grandfather Noel Burns was always nearby, encouraging, supporting and espousing Max's life message about being competitive and getting better in order to succeed.

When Nick arrived at Newington College in 1974, older brother Peter was already established at that elite Sydney school as a track and field star and speedy winger in the 14As. By contrast, young Nick was one the smallest boys in his year so scrum-half was a natural fit in the 12As rugby team – even though he'd never played the game. Schoolmaster Peter Hipwell described Nick's introduction in *Nick Farr-Jones:* 'He was just one of those kids you notice right away, who can do things in sport. You don't really teach them, it's more a matter of guiding them. Right away he knew how to run with the ball. He could step and kick, he had co-ordination and he really, really wanted to win every game we played.'

That will to win had already been demonstrated in the pool and would also emerge on the athletics track. At Miranda Primary School young Farr-Jones had won 'ugly' in the State Under 8 50-yards swim title in 38 seconds. His ungainly style apparently displaced more water than most of his rivals combined. In 1978 he finally triumphed in the GPS 1500 metres on the track,

'Right away he knew how to run with the ball ... he had co-ordination and he really, really wanted to win every game we played.'

beating his arch-rival Michael Ritchie from Sydney Grammar, who had always outsprinted him in the closing stages at past carnivals. Later, Nick described the wellsprings of that dogged will to win. 'I think you're born with a certain amount of competitiveness, but I attribute most of mine to the fact that I had a brother either side of me in whatever we did. I had to try extra hard to beat them.'

As a rugby player Nick Farr-Jones only matured after he finished high school in 1979. But that development was rapid. He progressed from the Newington College Second XV (he was too small for the First XV) to Wallaby scrum-half in just five years. During that time he began a law degree at Sydney University and became a resident at St Andrew's College, a free-spirited male boarding institution for undergraduates – at the time it was described as 'a finishing school for blokes'. He also enjoyed a significant growth spurt. When selected in first grade for the university in 1981 he was one of the biggest scrum-halves in the competition. His size at 1.78 m (5 feet 10 inches) and natural strength 85 kg (13 stone 4 lb) meant he could join a ruck with purpose or even rip the ball from an opposition forward. He also possessed genuine speed and an obsessively competitive nature, the by-product of two decades of intense sporting activity and backyard combat alongside his brothers Peter and Simon. Unrealised by all but a select few, Nicholas Campbell Farr-Jones was now a Wallaby-in-waiting. He was ready to take on the rugby world – and win.

Nick had made the Sydney University Colts First XV in his first year out of school and, after winning the premiership, was earmarked for the top senior grade team the following year where he debuted alongside his brother Peter against reigning premiers Randwick. But the Students faced a daunting challenge. The 'Galloping Greens' fielded all three Ella brothers plus Simon Poidevin. In Nick's words they were 'flogged like a convict caught with the governor's wife'. Nevertheless, his senior career was now underway and, off the field, all three Farr-Jones brothers were happily ensconced at St Andrew's College. But the University XV was not performing well. The following year saw the Students finish bottom of the table and they were relegated to Second Division.

That cloud of disappointment had a silver lining. Fortunately, Nick had shown enough potential to warrant his chance at a higher level. The chairman of the Sydney selectors, Bob Urquhart, had been impressed by Nick's performance for the Combined Second Division team and urged the Sydney coach Peter Fenton and fellow selector Barry Want to consider him for the upcoming world tour. The rest is history. Nick's size and strength then caught the eye of new Wallaby coach, Alan Jones. Later that year, on 3 November 1984, he made his Test debut against England at Twickenham. By then Jones had developed a massive forward pack and viewed Farr-Jones' hustling, 'whip-cracking' approach as a dream fit.

Days before the Twickenham match Jones had famously called Nick into his hotel room where the young Wallaby was handed a withering dressing down about his recent nocturnal visits to nightclubs and bars with teammates. The non-stop tirade lasted nearly 20 minutes. In his defence Nick said he felt

Australia claimed the Cook Cup against England at the Sydney Football Stadium in July 1991. An even bigger prize awaited Farr-Jones and the Wallabies.

NFJ receives the World Cup from Queen Elizabeth II.

he was performing at a high level on the field and, as a new kid on the block, the socialising was an ideal way to get to know his more senior teammates. That said, he also appreciated he'd been given a timely kick up the backside.

Rugby correspondent Jim Webster summed up Nick's selection in *The Sydney Morning Herald*: 'Australia has a big, powerful, driving halfback in Nick Farr-Jones (now weighing 85 kg) who, I feel, is destined to become one of the greatest we have had.' By his own admission Nick was on automatic pilot during the high-pressure game but fully aware that his girlfriend Angela, together with his brothers and mates, were all watching the match on television at St Andrew's in the early hours of the morning.

'The soft going underfoot also enabled Nick to work the blindside and two such sorties resulted in tries for Lynagh and Tommy Lawton. The record 28-9 triumph set up an unprecedented shot at completing a tour Grand Slam against the Scots at Murrayfield.'

Mum and dad were in the stand. The climactic moment in the game came just after half-time. With Australia leading 3-0 Nick fired a pass to Mark Ella and the set move they called 'Froggy' was set in motion. Mark took the ball to the line in a drifting run with decoy options offered by Michael Lynagh, Roger Gould and David Campese. Ella sensed the indecision in the defence and speared through the narrow opening for a thrilling try to help Australia seal a 19-3 victory.

After a close but convincing 16-9 win against the tenacious Irish, the Wallabies ran out in front of 67,000 parochial Welsh fans at Cardiff Arms Park. The signature moment of that Test is forever ingrained in rugby folklore. Australia's pushover try saw the Welsh scrum shunted and in full retreat over its own goal line. To suffer that fate against the upstart Colonials from Down Under was a total humiliation and left the home fans stunned. The soft going underfoot also enabled Nick to work the blindside and two such sorties resulted in tries for Lynagh and Tommy Lawton. The record 28-9 triumph set up an unprecedented shot at completing a tour Grand Slam against the Scots at Murrayfield.

The result was never in doubt. Before the game, coach Jones had a final message: 'Remember, there are four things that just don't come back: the spent arrow, the spoken word, lost time and missed opportunity.' Ella scored his personal grand slam of tries while Farr-Jones enjoyed special satisfaction from his individual effort when he took the ball from a quick lineout and beat two defenders to score in the corner. The Wallabies prevailed by a record 37-12. The victorious Aussies had taken their opportunity with both hands. In less than 12 months, Farr-Jones had risen from anonymity in Second Division to a full-blown Grand Slam Wallaby hero.

In 1986 Farr-Jones played all three Tests in the historic series win over the All Blacks in New Zealand. No Wallaby side had ever won a three-Test series on Kiwi soil. After being denied the match-winning try in the Second Test in Dunedin, the Wallabies produced one of their greatest defensive efforts in the series decider in Auckland. One stupendous tackle five metres out by 'Topo' Rodriguez on All Black hooker Hika Reid lifted their resolve to another level. With seven minutes to go Nick broke clear from a ruck, and then delivered a 15 m bullet pass to Campese who had been maligned after the Second Test loss. Untouched, Campo sprinted 20 metres to score the Bledisloe Cup clincher. In a moment of sheer jubilation, Nick then hoisted Campese over his shoulders in a 'fireman's lift'. Later that evening Alan Jones informed the team that Farr-Jones was his Player of the Tour and also the Players' Player. The journey to the inaugural Rugby World Cup seemed on schedule.

But the 1987 Cup campaign proved a major disappointment for Australian rugby. The team was sent packing by the French in a gripping semi-final at Sydney's Concord

Oval. A last-minute try by classy fullback Serge Blanco snatched a 19-18 victory. To make matters worse, the Wallabies were then pipped by Wales in the Third Place Playoff in Rotorua. In hindsight it was the most disappointing year of Nick's 10-year career in the Wallaby jumper. It also proved to be the end of the road for coach Jones. The subsequent lost series in Argentina was the final straw and Bob Dwyer was re-elected for a second stint as Wallaby supremo. He promptly named Nick as his new captain without even asking him if he was interested or desired the position.

But they had a rocky start. After losing the series to the British and Irish Lions in 1989, Dwyer 'bit the bullet' and chose three unknown rookies for the Bledisloe Cup Test in Auckland. It proved a groundbreaking masterstroke. That trio of Tim Horan, Phil Kearns and Tony Daly would go on to play crucial roles in Australia's triumphant 1991 Rugby World Cup campaign. Leading into the Cup, Australia enjoyed powerful victories over the All Blacks in successive years. In 1990 in Wellington, the Wallabies ended the Kiwis' unbeaten run of 50 games that included 23 Tests. Then, a year later, the 21-12 win at the Sydney Football Stadium elevated Australia to World Cup favouritism.

Although narrowly avoiding disaster against Ireland in the Cup quarter-final, the Wallabies confirmed their status the following week with a rousing 16-6 victory over the All Blacks in Dublin. The final against England was a battle of survival. The home team abandoned their 'kick and chase' game and surprisingly ran the ball, throwing everything at the Australian defence which refused to cave in. As the team's principal architects, Dwyer

A natural running scrum-half, he was always a dangerous threat on the blind-side.

Farr-Jones' swift, accurate passing serviced two of the greatest fly halves in history, Mark Ella and Michael Lynagh.

and Farr-Jones (despite his chronic knee injury) guided the Wallabies through the Cup minefield to claim rugby's ultimate prize.

On the eve of that final Nick had made a special trip across town to see his wife Angie, his mother-in-law and new daughter Jessica. In Nick's biography, Jess's mum recalled: 'He was as calm as ever I'd seen him – almost unnaturally calm.'

The deeply religious trio had a brief chat then prayed for a good outcome. Nick's friend Daley

Thompson, the dual Olympic gold medal decathlete, made a similar observation after visiting the team hotel. He recognised Nick's state of mind as one of total alertness. 'It's like the rest of the world is in slow motion and you're the only one who's got time to analyse every little thing that happens, looking around to make sure that everything is as it should be in order for you to win.'

The Wallabies underlined their world champion ranking the following year with a 2-1 series win over the All Blacks and a thumping victory over newly admitted South Africa in Cape Town. Nick announced his retirement after that game but was lured back the next year by Dwyer to cover for injured scrum-half Peter Slattery. He celebrated with a series win over the Springboks.

Nick Farr-Jones AM was inducted into the International Rugby Hall of Fame and the Sport Australia Hall of Fame. He left the game as the premier scrum-half of his era and set a world record for Tests played by a halfback. Nick also established an Australian record 36 Tests as captain. Always his own man, he stands tall as one of rugby's great ambassadors. As a player and leader, he never lost sight of the enjoyment aspect of the code and the need to strike the right balance between preparation and sacrifice. A successful investment banker and fund manager, he and wife Angie raised four children, Jess, Amy, Ben and Josh, on Sydney's North Shore.

As revealed in his biography, following Nick's first retirement in South Africa, Farr-Jones was presented with a gold Krugerrand and one of the touch-judge's flags by SA Rugby. At the official match dinner that night he handed the

'He left the game as the premier scrum-half of his era and set a world record for Tests played by a halfback.'

two mementoes and a hand-written letter to his late parents, Rosemary and Max. It read: 'To Mum and Dad, It's been a great day – a great nine years when we look back on that unexpected Test at Twickers. Thanks for all the wonderful support. Please put these two items in the cabinet back home to remind us of 22 August 1992 – the day we can look back on and say we got to the top of the rugby tree and got out! All my love, Nick.'

Australia's greatest ever centre Tim Horan in action during Australia's clash with Argentina at Ballymore in 2000.

10

TIM HORAN

Birthdate:	18 May 1970
Place of birth:	Sydney, New South Wales
Nickname:	Helmet
Caps:	80 (Wallaby # 680)

Australia's greatest centre, Tim Horan, was pitchforked into the Bledisloe Cup cauldron at Eden Park in 1989 shortly after his 19th birthday. That auspicious Test debut was the launching pad for a glittering career that included two memorable World Cup triumphs with the Wallabies. Tough, visionary and blessed with lightning acceleration, Horan effortlessly commanded the world stage. Despite a horrendous knee injury mid-career his sheer class always prevailed, climaxing with the Player of the Tournament award at the 1999 Rugby World Cup. He scored 30 tries in his 80 Test matches for a win record of 74%.

Tim Horan grew up on the lush Darling Downs in south-west Queensland. His father Mike was a handy centre and played two seasons of rugby league with the Parramatta Eels before opting to purchase a small dairy farm near Kandanga. With wife Helen and his two young sons, two-year-old Tim and four-year-old Matt, the family wholeheartedly embraced this physically demanding challenge. The brothers were very hands-on from an early age. Tim became expert at rounding up the cows, shifting the irrigation pipes, helping Dad fix the electric fences and even driving the tractor.

In *Perfect Union*, by Michael Blucher, Helen recalled: 'Looking back now, it seems a little strange, but they were very much like little

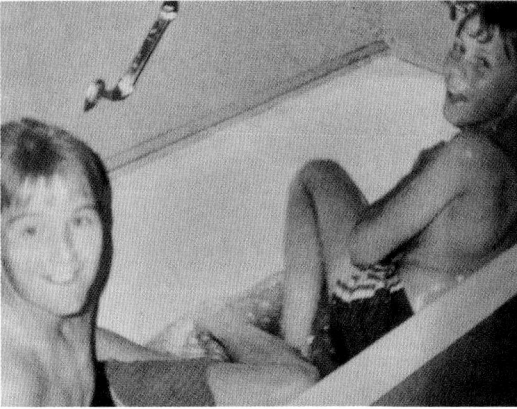

men. They grew up very quickly with what they were asked to do.' Tim's accelerated physical development meant he was primed for his rugby league debut with the Mary Valley Tigers at the tender age of five. The Gympie Times spotted his talent half way through the season. 'Pint-sized fullback Tim "Changa" Horan saved three certain tries, fearlessly tackling boys almost twice his size.'

Towards the end of primary school Tim became aware of another talented kid in the region named Jason Little who was a superb cricketer, spring-heeled high jumper and classy rugby league player. Their future lifelong friendship was cemented when both were selected in the Darling Downs South West Region rugby league team. Tim billeted Jason for a week at the family farm, introducing him to his makeshift goalposts and homemade cricket pitch (with accompanying hand-hauled roller). What more could two young sports-mad country kids ask for? A new football code perhaps?

Whether it was in action on-field, in a post-match bath or in plaster, Tim Horan and Jason Little rose through the ranks together.

Both boys had barely given rugby union a passing glance, but when they moved to their respective Darling Downs high schools, that all changed. With Tim at Downlands and Jason a boarder at Toowoomba Grammar, their familiarity with this often perplexing new code blossomed along parallel lines. Both were selected at fly-half in their school's 13A side, with Tim as captain at Downlands. Both were also picked in the 13A cricket teams, again with Tim as captain. They were still opposing No. 10s at the end of high school and when their two First XVs met for the O'Callaghan Cup. Fittingly, the result was a 6-all draw. Both were members of the Australian Under 17 team that beat New Zealand 16-3 and they also won selection in the Australian Schoolboys team in 1987. The exciting foundations for one of the finest centre pairings in rugby history were firmly in place.

After leaving school Tim had a season in Colts and, following a standout initial campaign, was named Queensland Colt of the Year. He went straight into first grade at Souths the following year. Suddenly things were on the move at pace. A stunning performance for the Queensland Under 21 side

'The 19-year-old had passed his biggest test. A week later Horan was on the bench for the Wallabies against the British Lions in Sydney …'

against NSW Under 21 in Sydney prompted national coach Bob Dwyer to select him in the Australia B side to meet the British and Irish Lions in Melbourne. The quality of his dazzling skills, speed, rugged defence, vision and trademark chip kick were unmistakable. The 19-year-old had passed his biggest test.

A week later Horan was on the bench for the Wallabies against the British Lions in Sydney, even before he had played a senior match for his home state of Queensland. Tim remained on the bench for all three Tests and witnessed at close quarters that ill-fated David Campese pass on his goal line that cost Australia the series. The tirade of criticism and vilification then directed at Campo had a lasting effect on Horan. He felt genuine sympathy but also took on board a salutary lesson about decision-making – and the incredible level of intense pressure that exists in the big moments of a high-level Test match.

Horan won 119 caps for Queensland and was selected for Australia before he'd played for his state.

Bob Dwyer reacted savagely to the Third Test loss in 1989 against the Lions and made six changes for the Bledisloe Cup clash against New Zealand in Auckland. He elected to blood three debutants: Horan at outside-centre, and Phil Kearns and Tony Daly in the front row.

Tim recalls the match was played at frantic pace and seemed to be over in a flash. The Kiwis scored a late try to prevail 24-12 in a tight contest but Horan had impressed in his first senior outing in Wallaby colours. Opposite number, the formidable Joe Stanley, came into the dressing room afterwards and presented his jersey to Tim who offered to reciprocate but was refused on the grounds that you do not give your first Test jersey away. Author Michael Blucher captured the poignancy of that gesture: 'Stanley's thoughtfulness left a sweet taste in the mouth of an impressionable teenager. He believed it said a lot about the game. Horan felt he had just joined a very select club, an international fellowship of rugby players. He thought how wonderful life-long membership would be.'

Two years out from the second Rugby World Cup, Dwyer and his fellow selectors seized the opportunity to initiate a batch of new Wallabies for the end-of-year tour of France. Horan was thrilled when his Darling Downs soul-mate Jason Little was named in the 30-strong squad. A month later their personal fairy tale became reality when the Toowoomba twins were united in the centres for the

first time at Test level. Australia's youngest-ever centre pairing, a couple of 19-year-olds, were selected to take on arguably the world's top pairing of Philippe Sella and Franck Mesnel in the First Test in Strasbourg.

Horan scored two of the Wallabies' four tries as they swept to a famous 32-15 humbling of a powerful French team. Australian rugby journalist Ian Telford was glowing in his match report in *The Australian*. 'Many hands made light work of the plucking (of Le Coq) but none worked more expertly than the two Queensland country boys who know their way around a farm yard, Tim Horan and Jason Little. The debut of the youngest centre combination in world rugby was nothing short of sensational.' It was the beginning of an extraordinary partnership. Horan and Little went on to establish themselves as Australia's most-capped centre pairing, playing 32 Test matches together.

After losing the first two Tests against the All Blacks in New Zealand the following year the Wallabies and coach Dwyer came under heavy pressure to salvage a result from the final match of the series in Wellington. There

'Tim and Jason savoured the victory by sharing a bath in their Twickenham dressing room, just as they'd done a decade earlier on Jason's family farm.'

was even talk that the coach's job could be on the line. Thankfully, the team saved its best till last skinning the Kiwis by 21-9 in a comprehensive victory. Horan was at his scintillating best in attack and defence and immediately became a target for rugby league scouts.

That win was a timely outcome one year before the World Cup. The verbal spray directed at Sean Fitzpatrick by Phil Kearns after the young hooker scored a critical Wallaby try just before half-time summed up Australia's resolve and fierce passion. Horan also kept skipper Nick Farr-Jones to his word and the pair stripped off and jumped into Wellington Harbour for a late-night celebratory dip. It was the start of a ritual for Tim whenever Australia beat the All Blacks on New Zealand soil.

Australia chalked up spectacular wins leading into the 1991 Rugby World Cup and unveiled some

special talent in the process. Future Wallaby captain John Eales made his debut against Wales in the record 63-6 victory in Brisbane. He and Horan eventually became the only players to start in two winning World Cup sides. Tim was at the heart of two momentous plays that were instrumental in Australia's victorious journey to the World Cup summit. Those triumphs came after considered forethought. In *Perfect Union* he recalled lying on his bed at the start of the tournament and telling roommate Rod McCall about some brilliant advice he'd been given by his dad Mike who told him: 'I reckon if you follow Campo whenever he's got the ball, just follow him as closely as you can … I reckon you're only one pass away from scoring a try.'

Tim reasoned that Campese invariably created space: 'If he's in open space, and you're right there in support, there's probably a very good chance you'll outnumber the defence.' In the semi-final against New Zealand Tim followed his thought bubble to the letter. When Campo regathered a Michael Lynagh chip-kick in the first half he took off and zig-zagged towards the line. The panicked defenders second-guessed. Campese went one

Top: Horan's acceleration and power enabled him to break through tackles. Bottom: Here he dives over for a try during the Tri-Nations Test match in Brisbane in 1999.

way, they went the other. Horan stayed in the slipstream, waiting expectantly. A final Campo surge to the left drew three defenders and then the magical no-look pass over his right shoulder straight to Horan was manna from heaven.

The other glorious moment occurred 28 minutes into the final. Displaying his immense skill under the high ball, Horan fielded a Rob Andrew kick on his own quarter and then bounced out of two hefty attempted tackles before darting up the right touchline. As the cover closed in he executed a pinpoint 'banana' kick that bounced and forced England fullback Jonathon Webb to run the ball into touch in order to evade the advancing Campese, who was just five metres out. Tony Daly's famous Cup-clinching try resulted from the ensuing lineout. Tim and Jason savoured the victory by sharing a bath in their Twickenham dressing room, just as they'd done a decade earlier on Jason's family farm. Champagne had never tasted so good.

It wasn't all about attack, Horan lifts Tim Rodber in a tough tackle during the Australia vs England Centenary Test at Stadium Australia in 1999.

Tim's career was now riding the crest of a wave. He narrowly rejected an attractive rugby league offer from top Sydney club side Manly of $200,000 a season for three years, plus car. Following a successful short tour of South Africa he then scored the series-winning try against the Springboks in Sydney in 1993.

But 1994 was a year he would rather erase. An attempted tackle in the Super Ten final against Natal in Durban all but destroyed his career. His left knee caved in, the kneecap dislocated, the ligaments ruptured and the cartilages were torn and crushed. Tim's knee was totally broken. Shortly after the incident, Little was wheeled into the medical room at Kings Park alongside his best mate. He, too, had ruptured his left knee trying to tackle the same player although, as it turned out, Little's damage was far less severe.

Tim moved to Sydney after his operation and lived with Wallaby physiotherapist Greg Craig and family at his Northern Beaches home for three months while wife Katrina and two-year-old daughter Lucy remained in Brisbane. Having just turned 24, Tim faced a daunting challenge to save his career as Craig devoted himself to that seemingly impossible outcome. Seven days

a week the pair made the drive to the Narrabeen Sports Medicine Clinic to forge what can surely be described as a miraculous recovery.

After an 18-month absence from the Test match arena, Tim returned at Port Elizabeth against Canada in the 1995 Rugby World Cup, again alongside Jason. Their previous Test together had been the win over France in Paris in November 1993. But Australia needed a Tim Horan firing on all cylinders and although he played two more games in that campaign (including the losing quarter-final against England), he was not at the peak of his powers. Nevertheless, Tim became the Wallabies' most-capped centre in 1996 against Wales in his 40th Test. New coach Greg Smith also made him captain in the absence of John Eales. In a memorable affirmation of attacking rugby he declined 11 shots at goal, electing instead to press forward to seek tries. Australia won 28-9 and then beat the Barbarians to complete a historic unbeaten European tour including the prized national scalps of Italy, Ireland, Wales and Scotland.

After switching to fly-half for the Wallabies during much of 1997, Horan was returned to the centres by incoming national coach

As incredible servants for Queensland and Australia, Horan and David Wilson say goodbye at Ballymore in 2000 after defeating Argentina.

Rod Macqueen. Dan Herbert was his new partner, with Jason Little demoted to the bench. The new pairing hit the ground running against an understrength England winning by 76-0, scoring 11 tries. Herbert, a powerful Queenslander, quickly established himself as Horan's running mate and the pair was instrumental in helping Australia regain the Bledisloe Cup with a 3-0 series clean sweep.

It proved a brilliant prelude for the looming Rugby World Cup in Britain and Ireland.

Tim played in five of Australia's six 1999 Cup matches. At 29, he was now at the top of his game. Despite a vicious stomach virus, his imperious form helped the Wallabies negotiate a challenging passage to the final. They prevailed in a heart-stopping extra-time victory over South Africa in the

'Herbert, a powerful Queenslander, quickly established himself as Horan's running mate and the pair was instrumental in helping Australia regain the Bledisloe Cup with a 3-0 series clean sweep. It proved a brilliant prelude for the looming Rugby World Cup in Britain and Ireland.'

semi-final before taking out the French 35-12 in the final. In *The Complete Book of the Rugby World Cup* by Ian Robertson, former Scottish international Andy Irvine outlined Tim Horan's crucial contribution throughout the last major sporting event of the Millennium: 'If defensive lines had to be cleared, Horan took charge and with either foot was capable of relieving the siege. He was a calming influence on his teammates, who knew they could rely on him 100% in every situation. He has great vision and looks so good because he seems more often than not to be a split second ahead of the rest in thought and deed. He acted as a catalyst in the knockout stages, doing his own job brilliantly and at the same time making sure he helped to bring out the very best in those around him.'

Tim's final Test was against Argentina in 2000 in front of 18,000 fans at Ballymore. Australia won 53-6 and, importantly, Jason Little was a member of the match day squad of 22. He won 119 caps for Queensland and finished his career in England turning out with London club Saracens for three seasons. After rugby he moved into executive roles in the investment and banking sectors and continues as a respected television pundit and newspaper columnist.

Horan was awarded an Order of Australia in 2009 for services to rugby and charity and community endeavours. He was inducted into the Sport Australia Hall of Fame in 2006 and the World Rugby Hall of Fame in 2014. His father Mike entered the Queensland Parliament in 1991 and served in the seat of Toowoomba South until 2012. Tim and wife Katrina live in Brisbane and have a son and two daughters.

John Eales's finger-tip control is on display at Stadium Australia in 2001 when the Wallabies made it six wins from the previous seven clashes against the All Blacks.

Birthdate:	27 June 1970
Place of birth:	Brisbane, Queensland
Nicknames:	'Nobody' and 'Slippery'
Caps:	86 (Wallaby #694)

John Eales was Australia's greatest second row (lock) forward – a supreme athlete with an astonishing skillset for such a big man. At 2.01 m (6 feet 7 inches) and 115 kg (18 stone) he could run like a hare, leap like a gazelle and physically challenge the toughest opponent. His hand-eye co-ordination and goal-kicking prowess showcased a complete package. A double World Cup winner and outstanding leader, his 86 caps produced a win percentage of 79% and included 11 wins from 20 Tests against the All Blacks. Eales was given the nickname 'Nobody' because 'nobody is perfect'.

John Eales first walked through the imposing gates of Marist Brothers Ashgrove, Brisbane, in 1980. A skinny yet strapping nine-year-old, he still had two years to go in his primary school education in Brisbane. The William Webb Ellis Cup, symbol of world rugby supremacy, was barely a thought bubble in the outside world. Cricket was his first love and a baggy green cap had already crossed his mind. But fast forward 11 years and history reveals a very different story. The tallest boy in the class had developed a powerful, elongated athletic frame – one that had catapulted him into the upper echelons of the grand old game of rugby union at its acknowledged home at Twickenham in outer London. Along with his jubilant Wallaby teammates, the now

Eales broke point-scoring records for forwards thanks to his goalkicking abilities. Here he has a shot at goal for the Queensland Reds in 1996 at Ballymore.

21-year-old was a world champion having defeated England by 12-6 in the Rugby World Cup final.

Eales grew up in a strict Catholic family environment in Grovely, a working class suburb of north-western Brisbane. His father Jack was a teacher and later primary school principal while mum Rosa had a full-time occupation raising six children – four girls and two boys. Grandma Nonna, who lived with the family, was John's spiritual guardian angel. She adored the two boys John and Damian, and Eales proudly acknowledges she had a huge influence on his journey to elite sport and beyond.

John was an outdoor kid consumed by sport-related activity. On the cricket side, Jack encouraged his son to practise and hone his technique. That meant the majority of his spare daylight hours were spent practising strokes with a stockinged ball suspended from the family clothes line. This practice graduated to hitting a tennis ball up against the back wall with a cricket stump. John's gifted hand-eye co-ordination was obvious at an early age.

Ironically, given his spectacular senior career success, Eales' schoolboy sporting journey was littered with disappointments. He tried out for state representative teams in cricket and rugby but, each time, the selectors found reasons not to pick him. But he did eventually make the North Brisbane Regional XI for the Under 12 State Cricket Championships in Cairns where he first encountered two boys who would become his life-long rugby mates. Tim Horan and Jason Little were playing for a Darling Downs XI, Tim as wicketkeeper and Jason

Ironically, given his spectacular senior career success, Eales' schoolboy sporting journey was littered with disappointments.

as their star batsman. Despite some subtle intimidation from the man behind the stumps, the gangly youngster Eales made a composed 40 and helped his side to victory. Nearly a decade later the famous trio would all play critical roles in Australia's stunning World Cup triumph at Twickenham.

Meanwhile, John achieved his cherished goal of making the Marist Ashgrove First XV in his final year of high school but again was overlooked at lock for the Queensland Schools team, his spot going to future Wallaby Garrick Morgan. 'Not tough enough, too skinny and too scrawny' was the selectors' judgement.

John emerged from school as a modest and reserved young man who enjoyed the company of his mates. But he was different – even taking his lunchbox with mum's sandwiches on his first pub-crawl. Rugby allegiance led him to the Brothers Club and he kicked off in

Colts I. When they played Souths, he came across his old cricketing rival Tim Horan who already seemed to be on another level to teammates and rivals.

Around this time his second-eldest sister, Carmel, who was studying architecture, was diagnosed with Hodgkin lymphoma, an aggressive form of cancer. The devastating news left John in a state of disbelief. Nonna led the family in daily prayer beneath the statue of St Anthony in the living room. Carmel fought hard and with enormous positivity through a long battle with the disease. Sadly, 10 months after she was diagnosed, she died peacefully in hospital with the entire Eales family at her bedside. John recalls that moment as the worst day of his life.

The loss of Carmel in 1989 seemed to channel a much sharper focus in his second season of Colts rugby and he finally made a Queensland team – the Under 19 Colts. His greater urgency and aggression on the field were noted by keen local judges including the new Queensland coach, John Connolly, who selected him in the State squad before Eales had played a game of senior grade rugby. Brothers played hot favourites

Souths that year in the Colts grand final. In a portent of greater things to come, skipper Eales kicked the winning penalty goal with time almost up. The worst day in his life had been triumphantly superseded by his best day ever on a rugby field.

His biography *John Eales*, by Peter FitzSimons, records a poignant and prophetic speech at the club celebrations by Brothers legend and oldest life member Merv Hazell. 'I have seen a lot of players come through Brothers over the years but I can honestly say I don't think I've seen one with more talent than you. I honestly believe you will become one of this country's greatest players, and in honour of that I would like you to accept my Brothers tie-pin which I have worn to every Brothers grand final since 1966.'

At the same time John was also selected as an all-rounder in the University of Queensland A Grade XI team and his cricketing future looked promising. Not only was John an accomplished batsman but his ability to generate extra bounce with his medium-to-fast deliveries set him apart. But in John's eyes, rugby union was the future and he made it his priority.

One year out from the second Rugby World Cup in 1991, the

Rugby World Cup winners in 1999. The skipper and his vice-captain George Gregan showcase 'Bill' in the tickertape parade in Sydney.

John Eales bandwagon was rapidly gaining momentum. He finally took the field for his beloved Queensland Reds, coming off the bench to replace his injured skipper, Bill Campbell, against Kiwi powerhouse Canterbury in Christchurch. His 15-minute cameo was eventful. Clobbered in the first lineout by the fist of rugged All Black Andy Earl, he bounced back and won four clean lineouts to help the Reds secure the victory.

National coach Bob Dwyer was in the stand that day and recalls his reaction: 'I thought: this guy looks pretty good. In fact I think he is ready to go.' The Brisbane referees certainly thought so. They voted for him to become the youngest-ever

Toutai Kefu scores the winning try in John Eales' last Test to clinch the Tri-Nations and Bledisloe Cup in 2001.

winner of the Rothmans Medal for best and fairest in the Brisbane club competition. The 20-year-old was then selected for the Emerging Wallaby tour of Europe. Team coach Bob Hitchcock was suitably impressed with his strapping youngster's performances. He told *The Courier Mail*: 'Eales is one of the most talented footballers I have ever seen. He has beautiful hands, runs powerfully with the ball, and is one of those great players who can reach the top without any nastiness in his game.' To cap a stupendous year climbing the rugby ladder, John was then named in a wider 45-man World Cup squad.

By 1991 John was simply unstoppable. Dominant displays for Queensland in their wins over Wales and England made his debut Test selection a formality. When his name was read out alongside Brothers teammate Rod McCall after the England victory, Eales' first thoughts were for his family and his late sister Carmel. Indeed, in the lead-up to the big game at Ballymore his biography revealed that Carmel dominated his emotions: 'Whenever he felt stressed he tended to think about her and somehow it calmed him, nurtured him, nourished him. He liked thinking about Carmel, and he was still thinking about

her at about 1.30 pm' (90 minutes before kick-off).

And boy did he summon all his inner strength! The Wallabies ran in 12 tries to record a record 63-6 victory. Four weeks after his 21st birthday Eales was named Man of the Match in his first Test. A week later in Sydney he was in similar form as Australia punished a full-strength England by 40-15. Coach Dwyer is on record as saying it was the best 80 minutes of football he had ever seen from a Wallaby team. All that now remained before the World Cup were home and away matches against the All Blacks. A fortnight after the England win, Australia despatched New Zealand by 21-10 in Sydney. The Kiwis won the return clash in Auckland 6-3 in a forgettable match totally dominated by the whistle of the Scottish referee. So, in the space of just four weeks, the young rookie Eales had already experienced a broad gamut of emotions of life as a Wallaby – from dizzy heights to a gut-wrenching low.

The 1991 Rugby World Cup saw a continuation of John's stellar run on the global stage although he did stumble out of the starting blocks. A serious knee injury to champion No. 8 Tim Gavin encouraged coach Dwyer to experiment with his athletic rookie. Eales played at the back of the scrum in the wins over Argentina and Western Samoa but the myriad of intricate back-row moves ensured it was not a natural fit and he returned to lock for the clash with Wales. Before the match the team was presented to Diana, Princess of Wales. John was awestruck. 'She was far and away the most beautiful woman I had ever seen.' The Welsh were humbled by 38-3 thanks to a comprehensive lineout eclipse by Messrs Eales and McCall.

In the quarter-final, the drama of the win over Ireland is well documented. Michael Lynagh's splendid captaincy and match-winning try in the dying minutes enthralled John. As did David Campese's mesmerising one-man show in the semi-final against New Zealand. But it was his own incredible match-saving tackle on Rob Andrew in the final against England that is most cherished by his teammates. Despite giving the pacey Andrew a head start, Eales somehow mowed him down just five metres from the goal line. Australia had won the Rugby World Cup avenging their heartbreaking exit four years earlier against France.

A successful short tour of newly opened South Africa took place the following year. Australia's number one status was confirmed with a thumping 26-3 win over the Springboks. For John the other highlight was a visit to a black township in Port Elizabeth where a group of Wallabies and coach Dwyer conducted skills sessions for hundreds of kids and then joined them for a lengthy singalong.

But our hero was anything but warm and fuzzy after an incident during the end-of-year tour of Europe. Against Welsh side Llanelli, an innocent attempted charge down resulted in an opponent falling on, and crushing, John's shoulder. He suffered a dislocation and a full rupture of his rotator cuff and was initially told his career was over. Eales missed the entire 1993 season but, thanks to the skill of leading orthopaedic surgeon Peter Myers and physiotherapists Cameron Lillicrap and Greg Craig, he was back the following year and at the epicentre of Australia's famous win over the All Blacks in Sydney when George Gregan produced his miracle tackle on Jeff Wilson.

The second Rugby World Cup in South Africa in 1995 remains a blip on John's rugby radar. An ageing team carrying plenty of injury niggles was no match for the hosts in the Cup opener. The stuttering Wallabies then worked past Canada and Romania but failed to fire. Their exit against England in the quarter-final came as no great surprise. A late 45-metre drop goal by Rob Andrew, the same man John had so heroically tackled in the '91 Cup final, broke a 23-23 deadlock. John did his best to carry teammates over the finishing line in one of his finest displays but history had determined Andrews would have his revenge.

John Eales assumed the Australian captaincy in 1996 under new coach Greg Smith. In all he led the Wallabies in a then record 55 Tests (later surpassed

Mum Rosa, father Jack, wife Lara and the Eales clan celebrate John's swansong against the All Blacks.

JOHN EALES

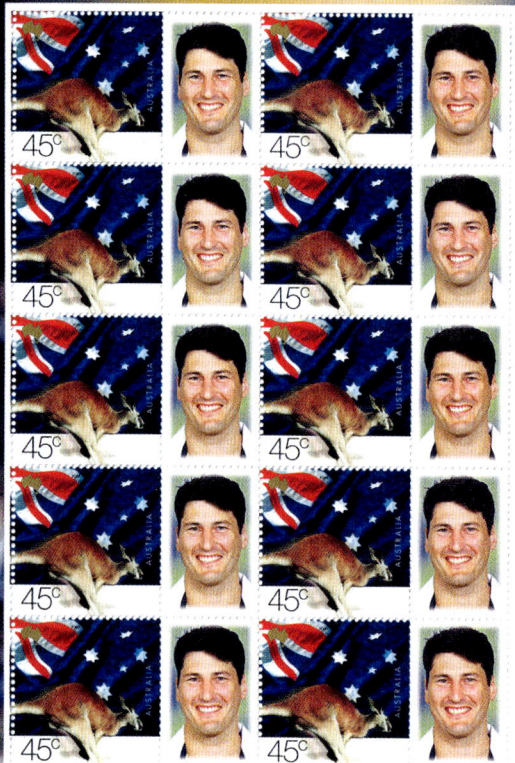

Australia Post released a limited edition stamp collection celebrating the Wallabies' 1999 Rugby World Cup triumph.

by George Gregan). He grew into the role to such an extent that he is now rated as arguably Australia's greatest rugby leader. His style was understated and by nature modest. His on-field deeds did the talking but so did his sincerity and strength of character off the pitch. His example helped lift Australia's performance to extraordinary heights, admittedly after a rocky start under new coach Rod Macqueen. John led his country to three Bledisloe Cup series wins including a rare 3-0 clean sweep in 1998. Another serious shoulder injury threatened his

World Cup campaign the following year but six months of intense rehabilitation, again under the tutelage of Cameron Lillicrap, ensured he was on hand to raise the Webb Ellis Cup in Cardiff in his third Cup campaign.

With Australia on the crest of a wave, 29-year-old Eales decided to continue and he captained Australia in 10 Tests in 2000. It was a vintage year. He led a superb comeback against the All Blacks in front of a world record crowd of 109,874 at the Olympic Stadium. Australia was down 24-0 in the opening minutes before eventually losing 39-35 in what was billed the 'game of the century'. Three weeks later in Wellington he calmly stepped up for the ultimate pressure goal kick. With the result and the Bledisloe Cup on the line and regular kicker Stirling Mortlock on the sideline, John's thoughts flooded back to his fearless match-winning goal kicks in the backyard – and more significantly that game-breaking kick in the Colts' grand final against Souths. From 30 metres on an angle, 'Long John' entered rugby folklore with the sweetest strike of his life. Captain Courageous, Captain Incredible!

Timing has always been a John Eales trademark and his retirement must be described as both picture perfect and pinpoint accurate. After leading the Wallabies to a series win over the British and Irish Lions, his farewell was slated for ANZ Stadium against the All Blacks on 1 September 2001. Mum Rosa, his father Jack, brother Damian and sisters Bernadette, Antoinette and Rosaleen had front-row seats. But with time almost up, New Zealand held a 26-22 lead.

Damian exclaimed, 'Mum we are not going to do it!' Rosa's response was instant. Clutching the rosary beads of John's late sister Carmel in one hand and his late grandmother Nonna in the other and then raising them in unison, she proclaimed, 'Yes we are!' Shortly after, Toutai Kefu scored the match-winning try to clinch a fairytale ending to a monumental career. Eales' 86 caps saw him bow out as the world's most-capped lock. He also made an astonishing 112 appearances for Queensland.

John was awarded the Order of Australia (AM) medal in 1999. Australia's Best and Fairest Player award, the John Eales Medal, was instigated in 2002. John and lawyer wife Lara have raised four children and live on Sydney's North Shore.

By 1996 Matthew Burke was the talk of the rugby world for the role he played in a number of special moments.

12

MATTHEW BURKE

Birthdate:	26 March 1973
Place of birth:	Sydney, New South Wales
Nickname:	Burkey
Caps:	81 (Wallaby #710)

A champion schoolboy athlete who transitioned into one of the code's greatest fullbacks. Explosive runner, damaging tackler and pointscoring machine, Matthew Burke was always a clear and present threat in Australia's No. 15 jumper. A stellar graduate of the St Joseph's College rugby nursery in Sydney, Burke scaled the heights of the code during Australia's most successful era in the late 1990s and early 2000s. He was a principal performer in many famous Wallaby victories, none better than his nine-goal demolition of France in the 1999 Rugby World Cup final.

Matthew Burke was destined for the sporting summit from an early age. Parents Maureen and Bob quickly recognised his latent mix of unbridled energy and raw talent. They ushered him into football (soccer) at just four years of age and Little Athletics at six. Chasing three older brothers in all manner of backyard sport also accelerated his early development.

Remarkably, his name still features in the record books in the NSW Under 7s 200 metres which he covered in 33.1 seconds – an extraordinary effort for one so young. Before high school, soccer with the Carlingford Redbacks was his first love but eventually cricket superseded his earlier commitment to Little Athletics.

The real 'game changer' was his parents' decision to pack

Burke holds the Tom Richards Trophy up to the crowd following the Wallabies' series win over the British Lions in 2001.

him off to boarding school at St Joseph's College. With absolutely no interest in rugby prior to the move, his sporting landscape was now transformed. As Matt explains, 'Rugby, cricket and athletics dovetailed neatly into the school year. Somehow I got through those six years – squeezing in three sports a year – without being injured. The old school in its commanding position in Sydney's Hunters Hill was the centrepiece of my life.' His track and field record as a schoolboy is unprecedented.

He won the GPS long jump and hurdles titles for six straight years. But ultimately promising cricket and athletics careers were jettisoned for rugby union.

St Joseph's College has produced more than 50 Wallabies but Matthew Coleman Burke is arguably their finest. Rugby is treated as another classroom at St Joseph's and taught like an academic subject. Matt's rise to prominence at schoolboy level was energised by the sheer quality of the sporting talent in his Joeys'

'Burke handled the transition comfortably, thanks mainly to his natural speed, high skill level and the inbuilt self-confidence and self-knowledge so carefully nurtured at Joeys.'

cohort. Among them were future senior representative rugby players Peter Jorgensen, Tim and David Kelaher, John Isaac, Scott Fay, Kevin O'Kane, Nick Ghattas, Graeme Thompson and Patrick Ryan. In Matt's final year, Joeys won their 44th Greater Public Schools premiership in 103 years scoring 252 points to 9 against without conceding a try. 'Burkey' played outside-centre and selection in the Australian Schoolboys team to meet New Zealand followed. Later that year he was joined by six of his victorious schoolmates in the national schools rugby team for the trip of a lifetime to the UK and Ireland. They were unbeaten and collected the junior Grand Slam against the four Home Nations. And, like Michael Lynagh before him, that selection in the national schools team dictated the direction of his sporting ambitions.

Following school Matt decided to undertake a degree in Human Movement at the Australian Catholic University – a logical step. So, too, was his decision to join the Eastwood Rugby Club, a stone's throw from home. Club coach Peter Fenton slotted his new youngster straight into first grade just four days short of his 18th birthday. Burke handled the transition comfortably, thanks mainly to his natural speed, high skill level and the inbuilt self-confidence and self-knowledge that had been so carefully nurtured at Joeys. Alternating at club level between outside-centre and fullback earned him a place in the NSW squad under future Wallaby coach, Greg Smith. By 1993 Matt was being loudly touted as a Wallaby in waiting. A strong performance for the Waratahs in their 29-28 win over South Africa earned a spot on the reserves bench for the Second Test against the Springboks at Ballymore. But he remained a reserve and his big moment was pushed back another week. An early injury to winger Damian Smith in the Third Test at the Sydney Football Stadium saw him finally take the field in a Wallaby jumper for the first time. Australia won 19-12 to clinch the series and Burke could complete the first of his 81 Tests in triumph.

For the end-of-season tour of Canada and France Matt was selected as one of four centres alongside Tim Horan, Jason Little and Pat Howard. But an injury to Tim Kelaher then forced him to fullback where he managed to displace World Cup hero and Eastwood teammate Marty Roebuck for the First Test in Bordeaux. But Burke required a needle and strapping and played with a sore posterior cruciate knee ligament that hampered his performance. Roebuck is the consummate rugby gentleman and team player. As revealed in Matt's autobiography *Matthew Burke – A Rugby Life* he sent a poignant note of congratulations to Burke before the game: 'Dear Matt. Congratulations on what has been a great tour so far. I know you will absolutely dominate today's match. I know you understand that what will seem easy for you looks inspirational for all who watch – so relax … Take 'em apart. Marty.' But what ensued didn't follow that script. France won narrowly and the injury he'd been carrying ended Matt's tour. Roebuck was reinstated for the Second Test in Paris which Australia won handsomely by 24-3.

Burke's versatility was becoming a source of frustration. His first three Tests were played at wing, outside-centre and fullback. He wanted to focus on fullback but injuries to gun centres Horan and Little the following year meant a return to the No. 13 jumper for his first Test start on home soil. Ireland were no match for the slick Aussies and thanks to a clever kick by skipper Michael Lynagh, Burke scored his first Test try. But celebrations were short-lived. Despite an injury cloud, Queensland fullback Matt Pini was coach Bob Dwyer's preferred fullback for the coming Bledisloe Cup clash with the All Blacks at the Sydney Football Stadium. Burke was excluded from the match day squad but kept on standby for Pini. The non-selection proved a bitter blow because Pini came off prematurely and was subbed from the reserves as Matt sat in the stand. (This was the match of 'The Tackle' – George Gregan's glorious last-ditch flying demolition of Jeff Wilson to save the game and clinch the Bledisloe Cup. It was the match and the tackle that defined George's illustrious career.) For Burke, the enforced spectator, it was a case of 'so close yet so far' from the thrill of personally lifting the famous trophy as a member of the playing group. Thankfully ample opportunities lay ahead.

'One of the best feelings I have ever had in rugby.' Matt's winning penalty goal in the 2002 Bledisloe Cup in Sydney.

Free as a bird. Burke's explosive athleticism was his point of difference.

The third Rugby World Cup hosted by South Africa in 1995 did not end well for Dwyer's Wallabies. A first-up loss to the host nation and then a sledgehammer exit against England in the quarter-final were heartbreaking. (Rob Andrew's 45-metre drop goal three minutes into injury time proved a forerunner to Jonny Wilkinson's much closer match-winner in the World Cup final eight years later in Sydney.) Despite the setback, Burke came of age at fullback defusing and repelling everything that was thrown at him by England's aerial assault. However, a final indignity awaited in Perth when the returning Wallaby squad came into contact with an Australian tour group who were flying out with the expectation of watching an Australia v. New Zealand semi-final.

Burke scored 29 tries in his Test career but none came any better that his sensational individual effort against the All Blacks in

1996 at Suncorp Stadium. The Wallabies had suffered a record 43-6 loss in Wellington but then displayed real character a week later with a comeback win over world champions South Africa in Sydney. Earlier, Matt had established a new individual pointscoring record with a 39 point haul (three tries, two penalty goals and nine conversions) against Canada. He was in the mood for scoring tries but is the first to admit his famous Suncorp 'smash and grab' was totally unscripted.

From inside the 22, the plan was to belt the ball downfield. Instead, the pass to Richard Tombs was lost sideways before he regathered and cleverly offloaded. 'The next 10 seconds or so added up to one of the truly thrilling moments of my career,' Burke reflected. In controlled support from fullback he swooped like an eagle, initially beating four All Blacks. As he crossed halfway into open territory with teammate Ben Tune in distant support, Jonah Lomu and Michael Jones pursued, Christian Cullen loomed ahead and Jeff Wilson was steaming across in cover. An audacious dummy to Tune left Cullen grasping at thin air and ultimately Wilson arrived too late. Channel Seven commentator Chris Handy effused: 'He just carved up through the middle and nobody touched him between there and the line. To me, it was probably the single most special moment of Bledisloe Cup moments that I know – to see that young man score.' Although the Wallabies blew a sizeable lead in the last 15 minutes to lose by 32-25, Matt had sensationally consolidated his ownership of the No. 15 Test jumper. His personal haul of 20 points also included five penalties.

Curiously, the hugely successful Wallaby tour to Italy, Britain and Ireland at year's end remains a neglected blip on Australia's rugby radar. That team is the only unbeaten Wallaby side to tour Europe yet seemingly few fans recall their success. Surely 12 victories including Test wins over Italy (in David Campese's 100th Test), Scotland, Ireland and Wales and a triumphant farewell for Campo against the Barbarians at Twickenham in front of 70,000 fans warrant greater recognition. Burke finished the tour with 136 points and, by season's end, had been named both *Sydney Morning Herald* Player of the Year and Schweppes Wallabies Player of the Year.

'The free-running French were shut down and demoralised by Burke's unerring goal kicking which yielded seven penalties and two conversions for a 25 point haul. A personal tally of 49 points in the two biggest games was testament to a decade of relentless practice and the search for perfection.'

After two years in charge, Greg Smith was replaced as national coach by Rod Macqueen who had coached the Waratahs through their unbeaten campaign leading into the 1991 Rugby World Cup. His appointment signalled the start of the most successful era in Australian rugby history and, despite dealing with career-threatening injuries, Burkey was front and centre to the action. Who can forget the night at the Melbourne Cricket Ground in 1998 when the newspaper headline next day read 'Burke 24 All Blacks 16'? His two tries, a conversion and four penalty goals said it all. Matt's amazing 'one-man' show was witnessed by 75,000 fans as

the Wallabies turned around an 8-0 deficit. Stephen Larkham had shifted to fly-half and the Aussie backs performed with new-found confidence and direction. The win was franked two weeks later in Christchurch when the Wallabies broke new ground with an 18-phase try against the All Blacks.

The Macqueen mantra of tough, clinical execution was now graphically unveiled. The Bledisloe Cup was back on Australian soil after a three-year absence. The Wallabies also took the third game in Sydney to clinch their first clean sweep over the All Blacks since 1929. But Matt's match-winning try seven minutes from full-time had dire consequences. As he strained to force the ball in Cullen's despairing tackle he severely dislocated his shoulder, an injury that required a full reconstruction. This was a shocking setback with the Rugby World Cup just over 12 months away. Fortunately he had leading shoulder surgeon Dr Des Bokor and 'miracle worker' physiotherapist Greg Craig to steer him back to full fitness but it took more than six months of intense physio to get there. But affirmation of his readiness only arrived a month earlier at Stadium Australia in front of 107,042 fans.

Australia thumped the Men in Black by 28-7 and Matt's individual tally of 24 points – comprising a record eight penalty goals – was a mighty statement for the campaign ahead.

The World Cup triumph in 1999 remains one of several pinnacle moments in Matt's superb career. The Wallabies were untroubled on their way to a semi-final clash with defending champions South Africa. It became a war of attrition and finally Jannie de Beer's late penalty forced the match into extra time. 'Bernie' Larkham then produced his winning drop goal which flew more than 50 metres. No-one saw it coming. Larkham was essentially a non-kicker who never attempted drop goals. But this one was never in doubt. The final in Cardiff against France was akin to a strangulation. The free-running French were shut down and demoralised by Burke's unerring goal kicking which yielded seven penalties and two conversions for a 25 point haul. A personal

Top: Matthew Burke in full flight at the Gabba against the British and Irish Lions in 2001. Australia took the series 2-1.

Bottom: Burke averaged over 10 points per game in his 81 Tests which included 29 tries.

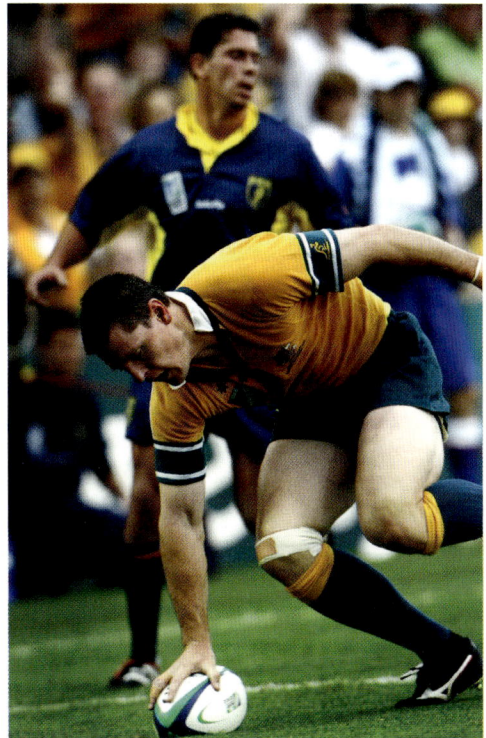

tally of 49 points in the two biggest games was testament to a decade of relentless practice and the search for perfection. Fittingly, Matt still has the match ball from that final at home. No-one deserved it more that day.

As a goalkicker Matthew ranks alongside the code's greatest exponents. His development as a young soccer player ensured his progression to the around-the-corner technique on the rugby pitch. At Joeys he practised relentlessly, able to access some of the best sport facilities in the country. Beyond school he became a disciple of English kicking guru Dave Aldred who wrote a thesis on the art. Matt did not fully adopt Aldred's teachings but he embraced

Wallaby powerhouses. Tim Gavin, Michael Brial, Matt Burke and their wives.

the central idea. 'Essentially, he wanted his students to be able to produce exactly the same kick, whatever the pressure situation in a match. The search was for perfection – to be able to produce the flawless kick over and over again,' Burke recalled. Unbeknown to the majority of fans Matt's left foot is bigger than his right. He wore a size 10 left boot and size 9½ right. 'I played that way for years,' he said. 'My right foot crammed into a smaller boot that leaves my toes calloused and bruised. By jamming my foot in for goal kicking I have the feeling of *actual contact* when I kick the ball. My boots are essentially the tools of my trade.'

Burke's 50th Test in 2001 was one to savour. Australia downed the British and Irish Lions in the Third Test at Stadium Australia in front of 84,000 fans. In the dying stages debutant lock Justin Harrison stole a lineout 15 metres out from the Australian line to all but seal the tourists' fate – which was also sealed by the seven goals kicked by one Matthew Burke. But if there is one defining kick in Matt's career it occurred the following year at the same ground. With the Bledisloe Cup on the line, he had to contend with twin

'I approached the kick knowing that I had landed many similar goals before. I hit it sweetly and it rose in the night air and went straight through the middle. It was one of the best feelings I have ever had in rugby.'

considerations: a vicious, swirling southerly wind and the fact that he'd missed five straight kicks from the same spot in practice the previous day. 'I approached the kick knowing that I had landed many similar goals before. I hit it sweetly and it rose in the night air and went straight through the middle. It was one of the best feelings I have ever had in rugby.'

Matt married his wife Kate in 2001 and they have four daughters. After captaining the Waratahs for three years he ended his career in England with three rewarding seasons for Newcastle after being poached by his 1995 World Cup nemesis, Rob Andrew. It's no surprise that he won Best and Fairest – a winner to the end. Matt is now a popular and authoritative chief sports anchor for television Network Ten in Sydney.

Always the facilitator and co-ordinator. George Gregan observes South Africa's backline alignment.

13

GEORGE GREGAN

Birthdate:	19 April 1973
Place of birth:	Lusaka, Zambia
Nickname:	Greegs
Caps:	139 (Wallaby #717)

'The Chosen One.' George Musarurwa Gregan was the consummate rugby general. He elevated the role of scrum-half from mere facilitator to conductor, directing teammates in attacking structures with precise timing and instinctive rhythm. His tenacious, confrontational approach was the hallmark of his intensity in attack and defence in the era of global Wallaby dominance either side of the new Millennium. The rugby world will always remember his try-saving tackle on Jeff Wilson in the 1994 Bledisloe Cup thriller in Sydney. His Test career spanned 14 seasons and four World Cups and included 59 matches as captain.

George Gregan's family arrived in Australia from Zambia when he was just two years old. An active child, he was sport-obsessed from a young age with a major focus on backyard cricket and football. This was hardly surprising given the elite sporting history in the family genes – his grandfather played soccer for Rhodesia. Like several other Wallaby Immortals, cricket was young George's first love and his junior football activity was in rugby league. But the 'live' telecasts on the ABC of the 1984 Grand Slam Wallaby tour of Britain proved the stimulus that steered him towards rugby union. 'There was something really exciting about being up late and watching the Wallabies beat the Home Countries at all those

The tackle. Gregan produced a try-saving tackle to deny New Zealand's Jeff Wilson in a thrilling Bledisloe Cup clash in Sydney in 1994.

famous rugby grounds,' he later said. 'Mark Ella was like a beacon on that tour with his inspirational play. I guess he was my first rugby idol. That Wallaby team was a role model for the emerging generation of young players.'

The switch to union was sealed when Gregan arrived at St Edmund's College in Canberra. Rugby was the main winter sport and George found a new hero in future rugby league icon Ricky Stuart. 'As a youngster I watched him for three seasons in our First XV, dominating opposition teams. My early days at "Eddy's" were spent at fly-half before I moved

to scrum-half in the under 14s. Subconsciously I'm sure I modelled a lot of my play on Ricky. He made a huge impression on me.'

Yet despite this committed involvement with rugby at high school, George still harboured ambitions of taking his love of cricket to a new level. To that end he was certainly mixing in the right company. At age level interstate carnivals his opponents included Ricky Ponting and Adam Gilchrist. 'Probably my biggest claim to fame on the cricket field was being run out by Ponting. I wasn't happy at the time but can laugh it off now when quizzed about my cricket exploits,' George recalled. 'I was lucky enough to play a few games for the ACT senior side after some success at grade level as a middle-order batsman.'

A superb all-round athlete, Gregan's finely tuned hand/eye co-ordination, discipline and attention to detail were best exemplified at another sport: golf. He was already down to a single figure handicap in his mid-teens, and in his first year of Test rugby in 1994 he shot an impressive one-over-par 73 in the Pro-Am at the televised Coolum Classic.

In 1992 George took a giant step on the path towards his boyhood dream of a full-time career in sport when he won a rugby scholarship to the Australian Institute of Sport. Although still a few years before the beginning of rugby's professional era, the demands of the AIS training program gave him an exciting new focus which helped accelerate his ascent to Wallaby ranks. National coach Bob Dwyer monitored his progress after admiring his array of skills at the Terrigal Sevens. Gregan's speed, toughness and visionary ball-playing repertoire had the undeniable stamp of a future international player. However, his debut in the Wallaby jumper against Italy at Ballymore in 1994 was eventful after he was accidentally poked in one eye, severely restricting his vision. His dream entry was nearly skittled before it had barely started. But it was straight back onto the saddle the following week in Melbourne as Australia completed a clean sweep against the tenacious Italians.

A first Test try in the 73-3 thumping of Samoa at the Sydney Football Stadium then set the scene for the Bledisloe Cup showdown at the same venue two weeks later. That gripping contest climaxed with one of the defining moments in George's illustrious career: 'Gregan's tackle'. The unforgettable moment came in the dying stages of the match that returned the Cup to Australian soil. It is now enshrined in rugby folklore. All Black speedster Jeff Wilson was airborne over the Aussie goal line and poised to score when George's impersonation of a human bazooka took Wilson out and the ball was spilt. It was a miraculous escape when all seemed lost for the home team. The late *Sydney Morning Herald* cricket correspondent, Peter Roebuck, wrote eloquently about the magnitude of the occasion from his London base. 'Two mighty teams

'When George was selected for the first of his four Rugby World Cups the following year the professional revolution was at hand.'

hurled themselves at each other and the thud could be heard around the world. And what about this Gregan character. He has the instincts of a champion. In 50 years, folk will sip their schooners and, as reminiscences begin, they will sigh: Do you remember '94 and Gregan's tackle?'

When George was selected for the first of his four Rugby World Cups the following year the professional revolution was at hand. Although still strictly amateurs, Australia's elite players held lucrative contracts which earned them around $80,000, officially to fulfil sponsor commitments and other off-field duties. Indeed, while the 'shamateur' Wallabies campaigned in South Africa as the number one World Cup seeds, the three major southern hemisphere unions were negotiating a 10-year US$550 million television rights deal with Rupert Murdoch's News Corporation. At the same time the rebel World Rugby Corporation was planning a global takeover of the code. After a short, sharp stoush which shook the foundations of the establishment, the Murdoch deal prevailed. Meanwhile, the Wallabies had performed limply in the Cup, bowing out in the quarter-final against England thanks to Rob Andrew's superb 40-metre drop goal. For George this was the last of his five Tests alongside skipper Michael Lynagh who announced his retirement after 12 distinguished years in Wallaby colours.

The onset of professional rugby prompted the creation of the ACT Brumbies franchise in the newly formed Super 12 competition involving provincial teams from Australia, New Zealand and South Africa. Under coach Rod Macqueen, the Brumbies were an instant hit and a host of gifted local players burst onto the scene to supplement the baseload of experienced interstate recruits. One of those rookie newcomers was Stephen Larkham who would go on to play a world record 79 Tests as a half-back partner with Gregan. The Brumbies developed a unique and very successful culture under Macqueen and subsequent coach Eddie Jones. That environment had a huge impact on George

A pro golfer in another life? A superb striker, George was a regular attendee at celebrity pro-ams.

Gregan both as a man and player. In his autobiography *My Life and Rugby* Jones cheekily noted the transformation of Gregan as he became a full-time professional rugby player. 'George had an understated, urbane manner which didn't obscure his ferocious desire to win. He was a great rugby player but, at the same time, the butt of constant ribbing from his teammates. When the game went professional, George shaved his head, started to dress sharply and

Clearance to Larkham in the epic Rugby World Cup final against England in Sydney in 2003. Jonny Wilkinson's drop kick sunk the Wallabies.

generally changed his look to match a superstar international player. Joe Roff always teased him when he pointed to George and said: 'See that bloke over there? I used to know him when he was a Kingswood-driving, Afro-haired, purple-suit-wearing physical education student. Look at him now.'

After an indifferent start in his initial season as Brumbies coach, Jones (in close consultation with Rod Kafer) totally overhauled the team's on-field modus operandi to create a structure in which the best attackers targeted the worst defenders. His gold-plated bonus was that Gregan, Larkham and Roff had emerged as three of the best attackers in world rugby. 'That was the exciting part,' George recalled. 'We were able to turn things around and win the Super 12 for the first time the following year, with new methods and a new strategy.'

Gregan and Larkham were the key decision-makers in that attacking system and their influence and confidence as a partnership weaponised Australia's whole strategic approach.

The appointment of Macqueen as Wallaby coach in 1997 ushered in the most successful era in Australian Rugby history. The Wallabies won every major trophy available to the 'tier one' nations. George played 38 Test matches under Macqueen for a stunning win rate of 80%. In that period the Wallabies won the Bledisloe Cup for five years in succession, won the Tri-Nations twice, defeated the British and Irish Lions and claimed their second Rugby World Cup. George rates the 3-0 clean sweep over the All Blacks in 1998 as the most significant achievement of his Wallaby experience. 'We'd really struggled against New Zealand since 1995, so it was deeply satisfying to finally shake the monkey. That series was the springboard for a very successful period in Australian rugby, culminating in our 1999 World Cup victory.'

An impregnable defence was the cornerstone of that Wallabies Cup triumph. The Wallabies conceded only one try, and none in the three finals games, which included their heart-stopping try-less win over South Africa. The 35-12 victory over France in the final saw the Wallabies hold onto the ball significantly longer than their opponents. The French tackled more and then were shut down on tired legs when they did manage to get the ball. It was Matthew Burke's clinical nine goals from 11 attempts that delivered the desired outcome for George and his teammates (notwithstanding the scrum-half's trademark flick behind-the-back pass for Owen Finegan's match-sealing try). 'The World Cup triumph was a different sort of elation,' George said. 'It's a very tough tournament to win. The team worked extremely hard beforehand and we were good enough to peak at the right time. With that kind of match schedule you do need a bit of luck but, more importantly, everyone has to be performing well at the business end.' On that score, every Wallaby player made an outstanding contribution.

After scaling rugby's Everest, Gregan had established himself as the world's best scrum-half. His partnership with Larkham was flourishing. They were keen to kick off the Sydney Olympics year of 2000 with a successful 'title defence' against fellow southern hemisphere heavyweights New Zealand and South Africa. But that dream scenario suffered a sizeable hiccup at Stadium Australia when a world record crowd of nearly 110,000 witnessed what was described as the 'game of the century' against the All Blacks.

Incredibly, the Wallabies conceded three tries in the first five minutes and found themselves down by 24-0 after eight minutes. Only a last ditch tackle by Gregan on Jonah Lomu two minutes later prevented that daunting score from blowing out even further. The Wallabies then engineered a famous comeback to level at 24-24 by half-time. George delivered the final pass for three of Australia's four tries in that half. Although Lomu ultimately snatched victory with a thundering try deep into injury time, the Wallabies were then able to bounce back with two famous away wins, both clinched with late goal kicks. John Eales' astonishing penalty in Wellington retained the Bledisloe Cup and then Stirling Mortlock's late penalty goal in Durban sealed the Tri-Nations and reaffirmed Australia's number one ranking.

The series win over the British and Irish Lions signalled the end of Rod Macqueen's golden reign as Wallaby supremo. He was replaced by George's second coach at the Brumbies, Eddie Jones, who anointed him as the new Australian captain. The Bledisloe Cup was retained five weeks later in Dunedin thanks to a personal contribution of 18 points by Matthew Burke. Despite a loss in Christchurch the following year, Australia retained the Cup in the return clash at

Leading from the front against Scotland in Melbourne in 2004. Australia won 35-15 to retain the Hopetoun Cup.

Stadium Australia when Burke triumphed again with a clutch penalty goal near full-time.

But there was no last minute pardon 15 months later at the same venue in the Rugby World Cup final. Jonny Wilkinson's extra-time drop goal was England's stairway to rugby heaven. Earlier, in the semi-final, the Wallabies had shocked the All Blacks with a master class in high-pressure rugby. It was a remarkable turnaround considering the Men in Gold had conceded 50 points to the Kiwis at the same ground four

months earlier. At full-time Gregan could not contain his emotions. In a high-spirited mix of jubilation and the memory of previous personal humiliation, George let fly with words unfitting on a rugby field. 'Four more years, boys,' he shouted at the All Blacks. 'Four more years!' he said, gloating at his fierce rival Byron Kelleher. Coach Jones interpreted the spontaneous outburst as the triggering of a release valve. 'You can say George was being cruel; but sport is a cruel business. I understood. George

Well done dad. George speaks to Charlie and Max after beating South Africa 25-17 in his final home Test in Sydney.

had been hurt badly, just as I had been, when we shipped 50 points back in July. We had suffered often against New Zealand teams – as in the 2000 Super 12 final when the Crusaders beat us by a point. We needed to savour this victory.'

The curtain finally came down on Gregan's amazing career in France in 2007 at the end of his fourth Rugby World Cup. New coach John Connolly had replaced him as captain with Stirling Mortlock, and even experimented with Matt Giteau at scrum-half in the two domestic wins over Wales. Australia disposed of Japan, Wales, Fiji and Canada on the way to a Cup quarter-final clash with England in Marseilles. Mortlock had a late chance to snatch victory with a long range penalty but the kick sailed wide. The Wallaby career of George Gregan, which had begun all those years ago at Ballymore, was finally over. His consistency was remarkable. He missed just 17 Tests across 14 seasons (which incidentally confined his scrum-half deputy Chris Whitaker to 48 full Tests warming the bench). Although there was no fairytale ending, George's peerless contribution had enjoyed so many highs. Apart from all the major trophies, there were other special moments to savour. In 2004 he celebrated his 100th Test in Perth by leading the Wallabies to victory over South Africa. Poignantly, his final Test as skipper produced a 55-12 win over Fiji at the 2007 World Cup.

Diminutive in stature, George realised he had to be in mint condition because of his size disadvantage. His longevity at the elite level was squarely down to his highly intense physical and mental approach. Off-field he was a perfectionist setting ruthless standards of professionalism and preparation. 'He was the most professional player by a mile,' said former Brumbies and Wallaby media director David Pembroke. 'At the Brumbies he was Eddie's general. He understood that good training meant good performance. He pushed the guys. If players made a mistake in training he would give them the "death stare". It was hilarious. He didn't need to say anything. They knew. Mistakes were few and far between, hence the success. His standards were very, very high.'

George enjoyed excellent stints with Toulon and then Japanese club Suntory before finally hanging up his boots. He was awarded an Order of Australia in 2004 and was inducted into the IRB Hall of Fame in 2013. He and ex-wife Erica produced three children, Max, Charlie and Jazz. George is owner and chairman of a global health and fitness company and is a popular resident pundit on ITV's ongoing coverage of the Rugby World Cup.

Stephen Larkham made no fewer than 102 appearances for the Wallabies between 1996 and 2007.

14

STEPHEN LARKHAM

Birthdate:	29 May 1974
Place of birth:	Canberra, Australian Capital Territory
Nickname:	Bernie
Caps:	102 (Wallaby #728)

Calm, elegant and elusive, Stephen Larkham effortlessly glided across the world's major rugby fields during a period of impressive Wallaby dominance. Although starting his Test career at fullback, 87 of his Tests were at fly-half with 79 of those alongside his celebrated Brumbies teammate George Gregan. Tall and lean in stature, he was a tenacious defender but it was his lethal ball running and spectacular distribution that drew comparison with Tom 'The Loping Ghost' Lawton, Australia's master fly-half of the 1920s and early 1930s. Stephen's career in Wallaby colours spanned an era when Australia captured every major trophy available to them.

Stephen Larkham reached rugby's summit on raw, natural ability. There were no development pathways or elite schoolboy selections on his CV. His was a 'rags to riches' journey based on pure talent – from honing his rugby skills at Lyneham High School, to third-pick scrum-half for the Canberra Kookaburras, to a contract offer from the ACT Brumbies and then full-blown Wallaby status. This was a rugby fairytale.

Larkham grew up on his family's fine-wool merino property near Yass in the southern tablelands of New South Wales. Famed bush poet Andrew 'Banjo' Paterson had lived in the same region as a boy. His much-loved ballad 'Waltzing Matilda' had special relevance for little 'Bernie' – jumbucks and

Thirteen-year-old Stephen (middle) in 1987 alongside cousin Todd (on his immediate left) who later coached a promising Nick Kyrgios for seven years.

shearers were a large part of his upbringing. A romantic might even suggest 'The Man from Snowy River' epitomised Stephen's free-wheeling approach. As a player he was fearless, bold and durable. Perhaps his fast-twitch ability to herd and corral rugby defences echoed the Banjo's grand mountain horseman.

Maureen and Geoff Larkham raised Stephen and his older sister Rebecca on 600 acres of picturesque Australian countryside. Geoff was a handy lock and No. 8 with the Wests club in Canberra where he played more than 300 games until

he turned 50. Stephen idolised his dad and never missed a match but, because he was so small and skinny, he was not allowed to play rugby until he was nine years old. Word has it that mum was not overly impressed when told little Larkham's first role in the junior team was at prop forward. His father still built a rugby field with goalposts for his son to practise his kicking, which he did endlessly.

The Larkhams were a well-known sporting family in the region. Geoff's brother Bruce and wife Stephanie were tennis professionals and built and ran the Hawker Tennis Centre which was just five minutes from Wests Rugby Club where Geoff and Steve spent most weekends. Christmas holidays each year alternated between the merino property and the tennis centre. Bruce's sons Brent (world rank 108) and Todd spent 10 years on the professional tour and appeared in all four Grand Slams. Todd reached 136 in world rankings and coached Nick Kyrgios as a junior for seven years. Stephen even partnered cousin Todd in the ACT Championships. 'Stephen's tennis ability was about the same as my rugby ability,' Todd said jokingly. 'He was very sporty and co-ordinated but rugby was his forte. That said we made the final before going down.' It did help that Todd was the top junior player in Canberra. 'Stephen was adamant he'd let the side down,' Todd recalled. 'Not so, and anyway he always balanced the scales at the farm and ran rings around Brent and I out on their rugby pitch.'

In 1995, future ACT Brumbies coach Rod Macqueen was aware of this 6 feet 1 inch scrum-half turning out for the Kookaburras in the Sydney club competition. Larkham played at outside-centre in the grand final against Gordon and, although the Kookas were beaten 24-11, Macqueen was impressed. The coach was convinced he'd found in Larkham the ideal utility player for the new Canberra franchise. The Brumbies hit the ground running in the Super 12 competition and injuries soon saw the rangy Larkham thrust into the outside-centre role. But the No. 15 jumper was more of a natural fit for Stephen who grabbed his chance when Rod Kafer was injured. Larkham relished the extra time and space to inject himself instinctively and to also energise the Brumbies' precise attacking structures. By mid-year he'd been called into the Wallabies squad and, on 22 June 1996, made his Test debut on the wing as a 'blood bin' replacement for Ben Tune against Wales at the Sydney Football Stadium.

Pat Howard was a foundation member of the Brumbies playing squad and Wallaby teammate. He vividly recalls Larkham's startling running and passing ability in those early days: 'He had a wonderful passing game and was quicker than he looked. Because of his lean build there was not much for opponents to hit which enabled him to be so well balanced in contact. He had beautiful hands, would take the ball to the line and pass and he

'Indeed, his sublime performance at fullback against Munster was a watershed moment in his blossoming career. Australia humiliated the proud Irish province by 55-19.'

developed a kicking game. When he initially moved to fullback, he just had so much more time and space to exploit his natural gifts. If it wasn't for Matt Burke's presence, I'm certain he would have also claimed "Immortal" status as a fullback.'

New Wallaby coach Greg Smith was also impressed with Larkham's attacking flair and selected him for the end-of-year tour of Europe. Although not named in the Test line-ups against Italy, Ireland, Scotland or Wales, his form in the midweek games earned him the Most Improved Player award. Indeed, his sublime performance at fullback against Munster was a watershed moment in his blossoming career. Australia humiliated the proud Irish province by 55-19. It was now patently obvious that the selectors needed to find a place for Stephen's exciting talent. In direct contrast to Burke, he lacked an effective kicking game but could still orchestrate lethal backline attacks with his uncanny ability to ghost through gaps and distribute flat, bullet passes. The win against Munster was the standout performance of the Wallabies' historic unbeaten tour in 1996 and clearly the passionate locals harboured long memories. Stephen returned to Limerick 23 years later as a senior coach of Munster.

With fullback Burke injured, Larkham moved into the Wallaby starting line-up in 1997 and figured impressively in their twin victories over France in Sydney and Brisbane. He was also at fullback in Pretoria when Australia suffered a record loss to South Africa by 61-22. It proved to be the last Test for coach Smith who was, by then, suffering from a brain tumour. The Wallabies finished off the year with a 15-15 draw against England at Twickenham and a thumping 37-8 victory over Scotland at Murrayfield. Stephen played in both fixtures but his days at fullback were numbered despite an exceptional contribution that included two splendid tries against the Scots.

Newly installed national coach Macqueen then had a very big decision to make. He needed a threatening playmaker at fly-half.

Larkham never shirked his defensive duties. Here in 'the match of the century' in 2000 it was all hands on deck against Jonah Lomu.

Ideally, this would be someone who could liberate his explosive set of backs, who was keen to get his hands on the ball at every opportunity, and who could knit a backline together and take it forward. The answer was right under his nose. Larkham was his man. As a former scrum-half, Stephen also understood the nuances of George Gregan's potent game and the pair forged an instant connection. Two incredible talents were seemingly 'joined at the hip' from day one with an absolute trust in each other. Rod Macqueen's light-bulb moment deserves to be recognised as a milestone decision in Australian rugby history.

Classic 'Bernie' Larkham leaving defenders in his wake against Romania in Brisbane in 2003.

The Wallabies opened their 1998 domestic campaign in Brisbane on 6 June by shaming England who were defeated by a record score of 76-0. Remarkably, Macqueen's reconstructed backline that day was the same combination that would start the Rugby World Cup final against France 17 months later. New fly-half Larkham scored three of Australia's 11 tries. Three months later the brand new Gregan/Larkham partnership had made giant strides chalking up nine Tests together and, in the process, completing a 3-0 series sweep against the All Blacks and a series win against Scotland. Stephen's haul of seven tries in his first nine Tests at fly-half was astonishing. Later that year Larkham and Gregan steered Australia to an impressive 32-21 win over Five Nations champion France in Paris. The most demanding season in Australian rugby history was completed with 11 wins and just two losses (both to South Africa). Stephen's first 12 Tests as Wallaby fly-half had produced 10 victories. The template for the coming Rugby World Cup was firmly in place.

Larkham missed the entire domestic season in 1999 due to a chronic right knee injury but returned in time for the World Cup pool clash with Ireland in Dublin. Australia prevailed by 23-3 and just making it onto the field was a personal triumph for Stephen. He'd left home with an inserted screw and cast on a broken thumb as well as a dodgy knee. He revealed later that the knee gradually got worse with every game despite intense physiotherapy three times a day and anti-inflammatory medication. The 24-9 victory over Wales in the quarter-final led to the epic showdown with South Africa at Twickenham.

Stephen's winning drop goal in extra time has been described as the defining moment in Australia's World Cup campaign. From 45 metres he calmly slotted the match-winner, his first drop goal in 29 Tests. But later, in a startling revelation on a *Rugby Australia* podcast, he admitted he had not primarily intended to go for the three points. Instead he was trying to drop-kick the ball over the dead-ball line. 'During that tournament if you kicked the ball dead it came back to a scrum from where you kicked it from. So, just kick it dead using a drop-kick. Whether it goes over is a bonus or not. And that's kind of what was in my head.' Bernie's each way bet catapulted Australia into the final against France which the Wallabies won emphatically by 35-12. Team doctor John Best was adamant that Stephen's courageous World Cup campaign, on one good leg, inspired his teammates.

After the Cup the Wallaby hero underwent surgery for the fifth time in twelve months. That operation was designed to properly reposition his patella on the front of his knee and thankfully he was back in full flight for the 2000 campaign. If there was one signature personal moment it occurred in the 'game of the century' against New Zealand who prevailed by 39-35 at the Olympic Stadium in front of nearly 110,000 fans. The Wallabies had conceded three tries in the first five minutes and were down 24-0 after eight minutes when Larkham launched Australia's counter offensive. In the 10th minute his brilliant dummy lit the fuse. A piercing run then left Tana Umaga grasping at thin air and finally, to seal the move, a 15 m left-to-right pass to Stirling Mortlock blitzed the cover defence. It was vintage Larkham. Amazingly, by half-time the Wallabies were back on level terms. The Wallabies bounced back to prevail in

Wellington against New Zealand thanks to John Eales' unlikely late penalty. They then made it a Bledisloe Cup/Tri-Nations double with another 'Houdini' escape against the Springboks in Durban. This time victory came from a last-second penalty by Mortlock.

The 2001 season provided the Wallabies with an opportunity to capture a unique grand slam of trophies. The Tom Richards Cup was at stake against the British and Irish Lions and would give coach Macqueen a fitting send-off. Larkham played the first two Tests but missed the decider through injury. Justin Harrison's lineout steal in the 79th minute, 15 metres from the Aussie goal line, clinched the series.

Steve returned for the Bledisloe Cup in Dunedin and played a crucial hand as the Wallabies achieved their first-ever Test win in that city plus a record four Bledisloe Cups in succession. His clever grubber kick directed towards Joe Roff saw the chasing winger grabbed from behind and a penalty try was awarded. At 20-5 there was no way back for the Kiwis. But one more triumph was needed three weeks later in the return clash at Stadium Australia. Skipper John Eales was retiring and, like Macqueen, he

He scored 25 tries in his 102 Test matches. This one against South Africa in 2005 helped the Wallabies home by 30-12.

deserved a hero's farewell. Again the Wallabies left their run late. Trailing 26-22 with a minute remaining, Australia won a ruck five metres out. Gregan passed to Larkham who took the ball to the line. He then subtly committed the outside defenders before targeting All Black No. 8 Ron Cribb who hesitated, thinking the ball was going wider. With everything now on the line we witnessed the skills of a master craftsman. Steve's delayed backward flick-pass found a trailing Toutai Kefu who then smashed through four defenders to score. Kefu won the plaudits but it was Bernie the

gatekeeper who had turned the key to unlock the All Black defence.

Australia's 30-man 2003 Rugby World Cup squad contained only nine survivors from the 1999 Cup final victory over France. Steve had overcome injuries to both elbows but the team was written off by most of the media. Coach Eddie Jones was under pressure after a 50-21 loss to the All Blacks in Sydney. But Jones and the Wallabies never lost faith. They were buoyed by their narrow 17-21 loss in the away clash at Eden Park where Larkham's intelligent kicking game provided few counter-attacking

Larkham breaks to set up the second try in the Wallabies' 49-0 thrashing of the Springboks in Brisbane in 2006.

opportunities for New Zealand's potent back three. The Wallabies were vindicated in the semi-final. Rugby league great Ricky Stuart made the jersey presentation beforehand and his message was all about trusting each other. In a major upset, Australia prevailed by 22-10 and, critically, Steve won a unanimous points decision over his much-hyped opposite number Carlos Spencer. Only England now stood in the way of a third Wallaby Rugby World Cup triumph.

Larkham struck early in the final to set up the first try when he hoisted a bomb towards Lote Tuqiri, aimed at exploiting the height disadvantage of opposite wing Jason Robinson. It worked as

'Larkham struck early in the final to set up the first try when he hoisted a bomb towards Lote Tuqiri, aimed at exploiting the height disadvantage of opposite wing Jason Robinson. It worked as the big Fijian soared towards the night sky.'

the big Fijian soared towards the night sky. Steve was also involved in the final play of the game – Jonny Wilkinson's extra time drop goal in the dying seconds. Larkham was the first defender to advance on Jonny but then checked when scrum-half Matt Dawson complained he was offside. The rest is history. Bernie's performance was heroic after being heavily targeted and forced off for 10 minutes. 'I came back on without knowledge of how we got there nor of any of the calls,' he said. England won by 20-17, watched by a record Australian television rugby audience of 4.3 million people.

Stephen played another 37 Tests over the next four seasons before opting to extend his career in Japan. Larkham's win rate at Test level was 68% over 12 seasons. He was in the winning side for five Bledisloe Cups and two Tri-Nations, the World Cup, plus two Super Rugby titles with his beloved Brumbies. He was inducted into the Sport Australia Hall of Fame and the World Rugby Hall of Fame. Stephen had commenced an engineering and IT degree at Canberra University in 1993 and eventually graduated after putting his studies on hold due to the onset of professional rugby. Life after playing has produced coaching stints at provincial and national level. It is certainly not beyond his capabilities to be Wallaby Head Coach in his own right. Stephen lives in Canberra with his wife Jacqueline and daughters Jaimee and Tiahna.

George Smith earned high respect from the New Zealand rugby public. His strength and resilience complemented a sharp football brain.

15

GEORGE SMITH

Birthdate:	14 July 1980
Place of birth:	Manly, New South Wales
Nicknames:	The Jackal, Camp Dog, Horhay
Caps:	111 (Wallaby #764)

George Smith was one of the all-time great open-side flankers. A supreme poacher at the breakdown, he won 111 Test caps spanning 14 seasons. He made his debut with the Brumbies in 1999 at just 19 and played his last first-class fixture for Bristol in 2019 at 38 years of age. Beneath his trademark dreadlocks Smith was a modest sporting superhero. Always a crowd favourite, his tactical awareness, incredible technique and robust physical presence commanded global admiration.

George Smith's Australian-born father Richard met his mum Selanoa after she'd arrived from Tonga to commence religious studies at Sydney University with an aim to become a church minister. Although she eventually graduated, her energies were instead consumed by the daunting challenge of raising nine children. George was the third-eldest of those siblings. Sport played a large part in the household. Smith first played rugby union for the Warringah Roos in the under 7s and rugby league for the North Curl Curl Knights. At Balgowlah Boys' High he was typecast as a hooker while his academic studies tended to take a back seat.

The future Wallaby's life was thrown into chaos after an incident during a school game when George retaliated for a teammate. He was found guilty of stomping on an opponent's head and the principal took the drastic action of suspending him. At the Year

A critical try against Ireland in the 2003 Rugby World Cup. Australia scraped home by 17-16 after a late George Smith breakdown turnover.

10 graduation George was strongly advised by senior staff not to return for his final two years. Rather than reveal the news to his parents, he opted to get ahead of the conversation by suggesting that he follow the same path as his brothers and attend Tupou College Toloa in Tonga. Although slightly bemused at this sudden change of direction, his mother agreed that reacquainting her son with his Tongan heritage was a positive move. In his biography, *George Smith*, author Rupert Guinness reveals that George travelled there on a container ship at a cost of '$200 and two pigs'.

The Tupou College Toloa experience was a life changer for young George. He had also received suspensions at Balgowlah High for various misdemeanours such as swearing, lateness and fighting. Although he didn't speak Tongan, on weekends he came to appreciate the simple pleasures and demands of life in his mother's village of Fua'amotu. During the week at college, students received their wake-up call at 6 am and were required to work for an hour before and after school in the adjoining plantation. Discipline and religion were a strong focus and by the time he returned to Sydney from his eight-month sabbatical, Smith had come to appreciate the humility and non-materialistic approach of his native culture. He enrolled at Cromer High School where he continued playing rugby while also turning out for the Manly Vikings on Saturdays and then rugby league on Sundays with North Curl Curl. Well placed to compare the two codes, George was adamant that the short passing and tackling of the league junior players were superior to the rugby union juniors. That said, after eventually switching to open-side flanker he decided he was better suited to union.

In 1996, representation in the Sydney under 16s led to national selection. In subsequent seasons, word spread quickly about this short-haired pocket rocket from the northern beaches. Three years later a belated call-up to the NSW under 21 side after an injury to another young gun, Phil Waugh, proved fortuitous. Smith was spotted by Brumbies coach Eddie Jones and assistant Ewen McKenzie who recognised a special talent. Manager David Weinstein forwarded video highlights of George's subsequent first grade debut for Manly. As a last-minute inclusion in that game against Penrith, he'd charged down three kicks and had five steals at the breakdown. The deal was sealed. Smith signed with the Brumbies under the nose of the Waratahs who signed his highly regarded rival, Phil Waugh.

The professional Brumbies setup in Canberra presented a whole new world for the 19-year- old from Manly. He had never lifted weights (and as his career unfolded, that aspect of training would never be a high priority). Nor was he keen on 'beep tests' – the standardised aerobic fitness metric used across all sports. Instead, George saved his best feats of strength and stamina for the rugby field on match days. As former Wallaby manager Phil Thompson pointed

'As a last-minute inclusion in that game against Penrith, he'd charged down three kicks and had five steals at the breakdown. The deal was sealed.'

out, in that area he was just like his Tongan mentor and hero Toutai Kefu. 'They never excelled in testing – it's not their game. They want to be chasing the football, not standing in front of a mirror.'

Smith's natural athleticism and enthusiasm for the game stood him in good stead when he made his Brumbies Super Rugby debut off the bench in 2000 against the Durban-based Sharks in Canberra. With family and former Manly under 19 teammates watching in the stand, his 20-minute cameo included three steals against Springbok Corne Krige and a frenzied effort to be involved in nearly every phase. He also played the last 20 minutes of the one-point Super Rugby final loss against the Crusaders in Canberra prompting a glowing response from assistant coach McKenzie. 'He scored a try with his first touch [he ran straight through new All Black coach Scott Robertson]. He had the physical strength – and we sensed what his potential could be with the right conditioning and training. He became a world-class No. 7 straight away.'

Smith's meteoric rise that year to Wallaby ranks vindicated the early call by Jones and McKenzie. When Wallaby coach Rod Macqueen phoned George to tell him he'd

been selected in the national squad, the still teenage flanker thought it was Brumbies prop Bill Young playing a prank. He responded (as revealed in his biography) to Rod's offer of congratulations with, 'You know what, Billy? You can go and suck my cock. Don't ring me again.' Rod did ring again and a sheepish George was relieved to hear that Rod's wife Liz, who had been listening in the car on speakerphone, could not stop laughing.

Smith's Test debut came that November in Paris where he was thankful to room with the experienced Kefu who kept him calm and focused. And what a debut it was. Australia won a torrid match by 18-13 thanks to flawless goal-kicking by Matt Burke who booted six penalties. George was named Man of the Match despite being sin-binned late in the game for a reflex high tackle. Earlier, during the Super 12 series, George Gregan had commented on rookie Smith's composed temperament. 'He was playing like someone who had been playing rugby for a number of years. He wasn't nervous. He was just a natural.' In Paris that night the same calmness and authority was on display. Smith was able to take the huge step up to Test level

George Smith and Phil Waugh were rivals since juniors who made their Wallaby debuts in 2000. Their friendship and mutual respect never wavered.

without any apparent effort – surely a pointer to his future greatness. The 'New Century Generation X' flanker had arrived.

In 2001 George was again a crucial player for the Wallabies against the British and Irish Lions in the deciding Third Test at Stadium Australia. On the day of his 21st birthday he grabbed his chance to repay outgoing coach Rod Macqueen who had chosen him a year earlier. A late lineout steal by Brumbies teammate Justin Harrison averted potential disaster but it was Smith's Man of the Match performance that provided the hard-won difference between victory and defeat. In concert with Kefu and Owen Finegan they finished on top of the Anglo-Welsh back row of Neil Back, Martin Corry and Scott Quinnell. Smith had a double celebration at his family birthday lunch next day when he was named Player of the Series.

Seven weeks later at the same ground George was able to experience the joy of retaining the Bledisloe Cup as a participant for the first time. His cherished room-mate Kefu scored the last-ditch winning try. Smith also won a Tri-Nations medal for good measure.

Desperation in the last line of defence against the Springboks at Subiaco in 2008. Australia won 16-9.

Earlier in the season the Brumbies had become the first Australian team to win the Super Rugby title downing the Sharks in the final. George had started in all 13 games and was named as the winner of the Brett Robinson Players' Player Award. After full-time Smith spontaneously presented his match jumper to Robinson who had retired the previous season. It was George's way of expressing his gratitude to his former skipper, the man who had embraced him in a fatherly manner since his arrival in Canberra.

The 2002 season saw the signing of rugby league superstars Wendell Sailor and Matt Rogers to union. It proved to be the last time George would hold the Bledisloe Cup aloft. Indeed it was a brilliant solo try by super-sub Rogers in the 60th minute at Stadium Australia that helped Australia on the path to ultimate victory and a successful Cup defence. Then, in 2003, Lote Tuqiri became the final 'big name' rugby league acquisition as Australia prepared for its World Cup campaign.

The Brumbies avenged their Super Rugby final loss to the Crusaders the previous year and it was George who helped his team to a flyer with two early turnovers. Both resulted in stunning tries in the thrilling 47-38 triumph over the men from Canterbury. Smith would later face many of those same Kiwi opponents in the Rugby World Cup semi-final in Sydney. Australia's upset 22-10 victory in that game saw coach Eddie Jones strategically employ two open-side flankers in Smith and Phil Waugh to stifle the Kiwis at the breakdown. In his autobiography *Richie McCaw* (with Greg McGee), the All Blacks skipper gave his take on the twin Aussie threat and their contrasting styles. 'Phil's in there at the breakdown every time, having a sniff, and is easier to control because you always know where he's going to be. George is much harder to play against because he picks his times. You lose track of him, don't know where he is, then – bang! – he's in there, usually when it matters.'

Coach Jones persisted with the same open-side flanker combination in the final against eventual champions England and almost pulled off an unlikely victory. That configuration required Smith to be a fourth lineout jumper. Given his lack of height the position added another interesting element to his already imposing range of rugby skills. Meanwhile, the perceived rivalry between Smith

'George is much harder to play against because he picks his times. You lose track of him … then – bang! – he's in there, usually when it matters.'

and Waugh (fanned by the media), had actually begun way back in the under 12s. But in truth the two players formed a solid bond and a deep level of mutual admiration. In *George Smith,* Waugh, who was a more confrontational No. 7, felt that George's best attribute was 'his ability to read the game – he was very effective because he knew where to be at the right time'.

On his journey to a century of Test matches, Smith missed only six games. In 2007 new Wallaby coach John Connolly even offered him the role of co-captain with Waugh, a proposition George declined because he wanted to specifically focus on being a specialist No. 7 and not co-share different roles. Stirling Mortlock subsequently stepped into that leadership position. When the 100th Test match finally arrived in 2009, George was beginning to feel the heat from an exciting newcomer named David Pocock. The media build-up had been exhausting for the 29-year-old Smith before taking on the challenge of facing the All Blacks at Eden Park – always a momentous occasion.

At the press conference before the game, Richie McCaw paid a special tribute to his opposite number. 'Consistently, he has been the best. Every time I've marked him, you know he's out there and you know you're in for a good battle. It's huge to play 100 Tests. I take my hat off to him.' In his biography, George relived the moment he was asked to lead the team onto the field and described his desire to acknowledge the crowd. 'Whether it be the Kiwis or the South Africans – but especially the Kiwis. They respected the way I played the game, so I've always respected them. I also remember seeing Jonah Lomu there and just giving him a little low five. I knew he appreciated the achievement as well.'

The Wallabies lost 22-16 after leading 13-3. It was a game they should have won and George blames himself after dropping a pass from Berrick Barnes just 10 metres out with no-one in front. That try would have given Australia a 14 point lead (the pass actually hit George on the forehead but he maintains he still should have caught it.)

Later that year, against Wales in Cardiff, Smith played what he thought would be his last Test. Selected on the bench, he came on straight after half-time when starter Pocock sustained a broken thumb. George then produced one of his greatest halves of rugby and helped see off the Welsh by 33-12. But at 29, and seemingly still in his prime, a distinguished Wallaby career was over. Or so we thought. A final season in 2010 with his beloved Brumbies allowed him to win the coveted Players' Player award for a ninth time. It sat proudly alongside his two John Eales Medal Awards, also selected by teammates.

A new rugby adventure then beckoned with glamour French club Toulon. George and wife Louise settled into the seaside town with their three children on a one-year playing contract. His most famous teammate at Toulon was Jonny Wilkinson, who had broken Australian hearts seven years earlier. The Mediterranean stint reinvigorated his lifestyle and, perhaps more importantly, also restored his passion for the game. From France, George and Louise, with their three young children Wyatt, Soleil and Ryker, uprooted to Japan to join Suntory

Short back and sides: son Wyatt (13 months) surveys the famous dreadlocks which raised funds for children's cancer charity CANTEEN.

George Smith on the scrum machine during a team training session at Victoria Barracks, in Sydney, in 2009 as the Wallabies prepare for their European tour.

who were then being coached by Eddie Jones. At the time, that three-year deal in Japan made him the highest-paid Australian professional rugby player. During this stint baby Rafael arrived in the Smith household.

In 2013, back in Australia, Wallaby coach Robbie Deans was struggling to find adequate replacements for injuries in the squad. Suntory granted a three-month release allowing George to return to the Brumbies and make himself available for Australia. That last hurrah arrived in the deciding Third Test against the British and

Irish Lions. But, alas, it was not to be a happy ending. The Wallabies lost comprehensively by 41-16 and Deans promptly departed. Smith had a further two seasons with the Queensland Reds in 2017–18 interspersed with playing duties in Japan, France and England.

George now resides with his family on Queensland's Sunshine Coast. For those interested in peripheral rugby trivia, he decided to cut off his trademark dreadlocks in 2006. Wife Louise performed the deed and the ritual raised a significant sum for a children's cancer charity. But one thing that

DAN
CARTER
INDUCTEE
#162

THIERRY
DUSAUTOIR
INDUCTEE
#163

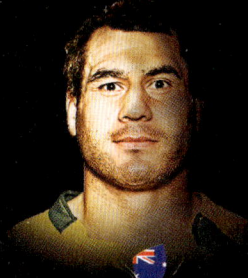

GEORGE
SMITH
INDUCTEE
#164

JUAN MARTÍN
HERNÁNDEZ
INDUCTEE
#165

BRYAN
HABANA
INDUCTEE
#166

Smith was one of five international players inducted into the World Rugby Hall of Fame in late 2023.

never changed was Smith's team camaraderie and love for a few beers with his mates. That social side of rugby – the fun – was always dear to his heart and Phil Waugh believes it was a major factor in Smith's longevity as an elite player. He captained the Wallabies on 10 occasions and was awarded the Order of Australia in 2014. George lists playing with younger brother Tyrone in Wallaby colours against Cardiff in 2009 as one of his proudest moments.

George became the fourth Wallaby – and only the tenth player in history – to reach a century of Test matches. He was one of a kind. In late 2023 Smith was inducted into the World Rugby Hall of Fame.

HONOURABLE MENTIONS

Spring-heeled Rob Heming outjumped all opponents on the 1963 tour of South Africa.

Reducing so many legendary Wallabies to just 15 IMMORTALS meant that a host of champion players missed out. The final choice from over 900 Wallabies might easily have included the same number again, all with genuine credentials for Immortal status. Their deeds are hereby acknowledged. Each made a unique contribution in the Wallaby jumper.

Nick Shehadie was renowned for his strength and toughness. His birth weight of 12 lbs (5.4 kg) was almost twice the size of the average newborn in Australia. As a big, bruising forward he moved between the second and front rows. Shehadie was the baby of the Fourth Wallabies to tour Britain in 1947–48 and his lone Test appearance was in the famous 27-14 win over England at Twickenham. Nick toured New Zealand in

Wallaby hooker Peter Johnson painted this tongue-in-cheek portrayal of teammate and farmer Jon White as a curmudgeon, hence the threatening bad weather.

1949 with Trevor Allan's Wallabies and his second row partnership with Rex Mossop was instrumental in Australia's first Bledisloe Cup win in 15 years. Shehadie captained his country three times and his decade-long Test career concluded with the Fifth Wallabies in 1957–58. 'Big Nick' was created a Knight Bachelor in 1976 for his services to public life (and surely rugby). He retired to private life in 1999 when his wife, Professor Marie Bashir, was appointed Governor of New South Wales. ***Birthdate: 15-11-26 Died: 11-2-2018 Caps: 30 (Wallaby #352)***

Paul McLean will always be one of Queensland's favourite rugby sons. The McLean family's rugby dynasty is without equal. Paul was a complete footballer and one of seven family members to pull on a Wallaby jumper. A specialist fly-half with admirable composure and beautiful balance, he was a decisive general with an unerring ability to steer his team around the field through his pace, slick hands and tactical boot. Paul was also a remarkable pointscorer climaxing with his Australian record haul of eight goals and 21 points in his final Test against Scotland in 1982. Despite his measured brilliance, McLean always seemed to be warding off challengers for his Wallaby jumper from south of the border. Ken Wright, Jim Hindmarsh, Tony Melrose and Mark Ella all forced the selectors' hand at different stages. A Test debut against the All Blacks at 20, 30 Wallaby Caps and a century of games for Queensland underlined his special status in Australian rugby history. *Birthdate: 12-10-53 Caps: 30 (Wallaby #571)*

Greg Davis was an All Black trialist who elected to explore his rugby destiny in Australia. His kamikaze mindset as a breakaway was an instant hit and he made his Wallaby debut against England in 1963. A wool classer by profession, his approach was frenzied with no regard for self-preservation. Davis

played all four Tests in South Africa that year and, together with Jules Guerassimoff, unleashed a devastating twin assault on the Boks' inside backs. Like Rob Heming, Greg was instrumental in the famous win over New Zealand in 1964 and the stunning victory over South Africa in 1965 and starred on the 1966–67 tour of the British Isles, Ireland and France. He was a permanent selection for 10 straight seasons until 1972 and captained the Wallabies in 16 Tests over the last four years of his career. Greg always set the sportsmanship bar at the highest level. He died of a brain tumour in 1979. *Birthdate: 27-7-39 Died: 24-7-79 Caps: 39 (Wallaby #485)*

Jonathon White was a powerful specialist loose-head prop who grew up on family farms at Cumnock and Yeoval in central western New South Wales. His outstanding performance for Central West in their shock win over the New Zealand Maori in 1958 earned White a spot in the NSW team and Test selection then followed against the All Blacks. He took on the best front-row exponents and was never mastered. Jon performed mighty deeds against the massive Springbok scrum in 1963. His technical expertise alongside fellow front-rowers Peter Johnson and John Thornett was instrumental in Australia's dramatic revival in the 1960s. As a former second-rower, he also jumped at the front of the lineout and was a fine cover defender. 'Noja' was a driving force in the rising stocks of NSW Country and finished his Wallaby career in style with a record 20-5 win over New Zealand in Wellington in 1964 and the home series victory against South Africa the following year. *Birthdate: 27-2-35 Caps: 24 (Wallaby #449)*

Phil Kearns was the prototype of a modern day hooker. He had the size and strength of a front-rower with the athleticism and mobility of a skilful back-rower. Kearns was a bold selection by Wallaby coach Bob Dwyer in 1989 when chosen straight from Randwick's reserve grade to face the All Blacks at Eden Park in the first of his 67 Tests. He then scored Australia's only try in the memorable victory over the All Blacks in Wellington. 1990 was the start of his record-breaking front-row partnership across 36 Tests with Tony Daly and Ewen McKenzie – all up he started a record 43 Tests with McKenzie. Phil was a key member of Australia's victorious World Cup team in 1991 and was selected again for the Cup in 1995 and 1999 when the Wallabies triumphed for a second time. Captaining the Wallabies on 10 occasions over an 11-year span, he led Australia to their series win over South Africa in 1993. *Birthdate: 27-6-67 Caps: 67 (Wallaby #681)*

William 'Wild Bill' Cerutti, the son of an Italian immigrant, made a winning 'Test' debut as a 19-year-old against the All Blacks on the 1928 Waratahs tour of New Zealand. He earned a fearsome reputation as a tough and abrasive prop forward who never took a backward step. His big break arrived when selected to play for The Rest against the returning 1927–28 Waratahs. Bill ignored reputations and tackled with a ferocity, prompting a spectator to enquire, 'Who's that wild bastard out there?' The comment was picked up by a journalist and the nickname stuck. Bill's 21 Tests spanned a decade and included milestone victories over the All Blacks (including the 3-0 series sweep in 1929) and Springboks. Cerutti played his rugby in a confrontational manner and won a reputation in New Zealand as the most popular

Australian player ever to tour there. He managed the Wallabies on their historic tour of NZ in 1949 when Australia regained the Bledisloe Cup after a 15 year absence. ***Birthdate: 7-5-09 Died: 3-7-65 Caps: 21 (Wallaby #246)***

Graham Cooke is rightly celebrated as the toughest and most durable lock to ever pull on a Wallaby jumper. Born in 1912 at Nanango near Kingaroy, he was a freakish specimen for a big man and a self-described 'wowser' because he did not drink or smoke. His rippling frame (6 feet 3 inches/1.9 m and 15 stone/95 kg) allowed him to match the best second rowers in the game. In *Wallaby Greats* Max Howell noted, 'He had a right hand that could have graced the boxing rings of the world.' A late starter in rugby at 18 he made his winning Test debut as a 20-year-old against the All Blacks in 1932 at the SCG. An automatic selection for the 1933 tour of South Africa, he dominated the lineout in Australia's shock 21-6 win over the Springboks in Durban. Incredibly, 14 years later and aged 35, he started all five Tests as principal lineout jumper on the 1947–48 Wallaby tour to Europe and was adjudged Australia's

best 'tight' forward. ***Birthdate: 2-1-12 Died: 24-5-96 Caps: 13 (Wallaby #278)***

Tony Shaw relished his reputation as an 'enforcer'. A member of the renowned Brothers Club his toughness was legendary and his strength at ruck and maul was his standout feature. Shaw won state and Australian honours at 20 and his marauding back-row combination with Queensland teammates Mark Loane and Greg Cornelsen demolished opponents. He played in all four Tests on the 1975–76 Wallaby tour of Britain and in 1978 led the Wallabies to New Zealand where they recorded their famous 30-16 Test victory at Eden Park. Tony was a standout in Australia's Bledisloe Cup triumphs in 1979 and 1980 and – with Cornelsen, Peter McLean and Brendan Moon – formed a select quartet who beat the All Blacks in four of five straight Tests. Shaw retained the captaincy for the major 1981–82 British tour and retired as a winner at the SCG against the Scots in 1982. ***Birthdate: 23-3-53 Caps: 36 (Wallaby #565)***

Joe Roff, the celebrated ACT winger, played soccer until he was 14. But after switching codes he quickly became a dominant rugby player at all junior levels. His effortless, explosive running and imposing size and power (6 feet 3 inches/1.9 m and 16 stone/102 kg) soon stamped him as an automatic Test selection. Roff made his Test debut at 19 against Canada at the 1995 Rugby World Cup and from late 1996 to 2001 started a record 62 consecutive Tests. During that period the Wallabies won four Bledisloe Cups, two Tri-Nations and the 1999 Rugby World Cup. He scored 30 Test tries, none more critical than his series-turning double against the British and Irish Lions in Melbourne in 2001. Trailing 11-3 at half-time, he poached a looped pass from Jonny Wilkinson and out-sped the defence in a thrilling 40 m dash. His 86 caps included three World Cups in a 10-year Wallaby career. ***Birthdate: 20-9-75 Caps: 86 (Wallaby #719)***

Greg Cornelsen is enshrined in rugby history as the only man to score four tries against the All Blacks in a single Test match. Tall and bearded, he emerged in the wonderful NSW Country team of the mid-1970s under innovative coach Daryl Haberecht. Greg then moved to Queensland where his combination with Tony Shaw and Mark Loane terrorised all comers. He made his Wallaby debut against New Zealand in 1974 in the 16-16 draw at Ballymore and became a permanent fixture for the next eight seasons. 'Corney' alternated between flanker and No. 8 and reserved his finest performances for the Bledisloe Cup, his last five Tests against the All Blacks produced four fabulous wins. In 1978 he was named as one of NZ's five Players of the Year in the *DB Rugby Annual*. Editor Bob Howitt described Greg as follows: 'One of the most talented and constructive No. 8s to tour New Zealand. Fast and strong he got through a terrific amount of ball with minimum effort and maximum efficiency.' ***Birthdate: 29-8-52 Caps: 25 (Wallaby #574)***

Tommy Lawton, a Rhodes Scholar and one of the game's greatest five-eighths, was known as 'The Loping Ghost' because of his tall, lean build and deceptive long stride. Although an advocate of running rugby, his peerless kicking game was a brilliant adjunct to his ball-handling repertoire. He won rave reviews on the acclaimed 1927–28 Waratahs tour of Europe playing in 27 of the 31 games. In

1929 he captained the Wallabies to a historic 3-0 series win over the All Blacks and, the following year, led them to victory over the British Isles. His calmness, the trademark body swerve emanating from powerful hips and his cultured handling were embodied in his hard, compact six-foot frame. A sportsman of freakish all-round talent, he was selected for the Queensland rugby union team in 1917 while still attending Brisbane Grammar School. *Birthdate: 16-1-1899 Died: 28-6-78 Caps: 14 (Wallaby #154)*

Tommy 'Turtle' Lawton (Jnr) was the grandson of the 1929–30 Wallaby captain of the same name. He played 41 Tests and upheld the family's notable deeds on the rugby field. A compact 'man mountain' who tipped the scales at 111 kg (17.5 stone), he gave Australia's scrum unprecedented traction on the Grand Slam Wallaby tour in 1984. Packing down between Enrique 'Topo' Rodriguez and Andy McIntyre with Steve Cutler and Steve Williams in behind, the Wallabies fielded the biggest forward pack in their history. On that tour, Tommy emulated the winning feat at Cardiff Arms Park of his famous grandfather 57 years earlier. Australia's celebrated pushover try in that game warranted a spiritual tribute to Tom Snr who had died in 1978. In a spontaneous release of pride after full-time, Tom Jnr crouched on all fours and kissed the hallowed turf. Lawton was a massive force in Australia's historic three-Test series win against the 1986 All Blacks in New Zealand. *Birthdate: 27-11-62 Caps: 41 (Wallaby #639)*

John Hipwell played at the top level of rugby for 16 years and established himself as the greatest scrum-half of his era. Raised in Newcastle he played for the Waratahs club where he was mentored by famous Wallaby scrum-half Cyril Burke. As an 18-year-old understudy to the great Ken Catchpole on the 1967–68 tour of UK, France and Canada, he made his Test debut when 'Catchy' suffered a horrendous groin injury against the All Blacks at the SCG. Diminutive and stocky in build his cover defence was legendary. Hipwell had a beautiful wristy pass and was devastating on the break. Despite playing behind losing forward packs, his class never dimmed, although winning just 11 of his 36 Tests. 'Hippy' embarked on three major tours to Britain, leading the squad in 1975-76, and was the lynchpin of Australia's attack when Greg Cornelsen scored his four tries against the Kiwis. ***Birthdate: 24-1-48 Died: 23-9-2013 Caps: 36 (Wallaby #519)***

Mark Loane ranks alongside Australia's greatest No. 8 forwards. In his prime his on-field presence resembled a runaway freight train, hurtling at breakneck pace in attack and defence and ready to obliterate anything in his path. Loane's 10-year Test career began when he became the youngest Wallaby forward debutant in 37 years when blooded at 18 against Tonga in 1973. His upper body resembled a chiselled slab of granite while his speed off the mark was electric. Mark was a key figure in the resurgence of Queensland rugby in the mid-1970s. He made two major Wallaby tours to Britain, starred against touring Wales in the 2-0 series win in 1978 and captained Australia to their drought-breaking Bledisloe Cup victory at the SCG in 1979. Loane played a significant role in Australia's rugby journey back to self-respect. He bowed out with a record win against Scotland in Sydney in 1982, as captain. ***Birthdate: 11-7-54 Caps: 28 (Wallaby #560)***

Andrew Slack – 'Mr Dependable' – led Australia to Grand Slam glory in Britain and Ireland in 1984 and the historic Bledisloe Cup series win on New Zealand soil in 1986. 'Slacky' was a specialist outside-centre and the consummate team player. His outstanding natural athletic ability was often understated but he helped those around him look even better through his strategic football brain and deft running and passing. Andrew made his debut in the winning home series against the Welsh in 1978 and was again prominent the following year at the SCG when Australia regained the Bledisloe Cup. Slack's career blossomed when he assumed the Wallaby captaincy from Mark Ella in 1984, winning 14 of 19 Tests as skipper. Calm, humble and resourceful on and off the field, his 'silk glove' approach was the perfect foil for enigmatic and feisty national coach Alan Jones. He played 133 times for Queensland. ***Birthdate: 24-9-55 Caps: 39 (Wallaby #595)***

Rob Heming's performances on the 1963 tour of South Africa stamped him as one of the greatest lineout jumpers of all time. He was not a big lock but he was brave and could leap like a cougar. After touring South Africa in 1961 Rob realised he needed to strengthen so he worked at the gym from 5 am every day with special emphasis on his calves. That dedication paid off and in 1963 the Wallabies were able to out-jump and out-smart the Springboks in the critical lineout battle. The Third Test win for the Wallabies at Ellis Park meant the Boks had lost successive home Tests for the first time since 1896. Rob and his teammates then backed up with a record-breaking 20-5 victory over the All Blacks in Wellington the next year and a historic home series win over South Africa in 1965. The Wallabies' first-ever win over Wales in 1967 was achieved despite Rob playing with a broken foot. The Welsh crowd spontaneously burst into song with 'Waltzing Matilda' at full-time. ***Birthdate: 11-12-32 Died: 7-1-2023 Caps: 21 (Wallaby: #466)***

Peter Johnson was a lightning striker with a low centre of gravity allowing him to consistently pinch opposition scrum feeds. His extraordinary career as Wallaby hooker extended over 13 seasons from 1959 to 1972 when he became the national record holder on 42 caps. Johnson formed one of Australia's greatest front-row combinations with John Thornett and Jon White. Swift and constructive around the field, his scrum technique enabled him to develop an uncanny understanding with scrum-half Ken Catchpole which helped ensure quick delivery to the backs. The pair made a huge statement when first united in NSW's 18-14 win against the 1959 British Lions. His finest wins included the back-to-back victories over South Africa in 1963, the record win over NZ in Wellington in 1964, the first-ever series triumph over the Springboks two years later and the famous results against Wales and England on the 1966-67 tour. He played a record 37 consecutive Tests including five as captain and overall played 92 games for his country. ***Birthdate: 13-9-36 Died: 12-7-2016 Caps: 42 (Wallaby #453)***

Skipper Mark Loane does an SCG lap of honour with Geoff Shaw on left, Tony Melrose and Tony Shaw after regaining the Bledisloe Cup in 1979.

Phil Kearns was a member of Australia's Rugby World Cup-winning teams of 1991 and 1999.

THE ALL-TIME WALLABY TEAM

Significantly, all selected players were prominent in golden eras of Australian Rugby. The starting team has seven World Cup winners and eight players who were exclusively from the amateur era. Every member of the backline achieved 'world XV status' while the forward pack has a careful blend of high skill, mobility and aggression. Eight members of the starting team captained Australia at Test level. Readers may query why Immortal John Thornett missed a front-row starting spot. The answer is that he only moved permanently to tight-head prop for his last 11 Tests. He spent his first five years in the back row before shifting to the second row for his next 10 Test matches.

Matt Burke wins the fullback berth ahead of Roger Gould, Jim Lenehan and Alec Ross based on his explosive athleticism in attack and defence and his match-winning goalkicking. Joe Roff brings size, skill and pace on one wing and gets the nod over Brendan Moon while David Campese, my greatest entertainer ever, picks himself

on the other. Cyril Towers wins outside-centre narrowly over Trevor Allan. His famous ability to set up his wingers and always create space for his supports secured my vote. Like Campese, Tim Horan picks himself and has a mortgage on the No. 12 jumper. Fly-half goes to Mark Ella over Michael Lynagh and Stephen Larkham. His peerless catch/pass/support skillset would turbo charge this backline, especially with the brilliant service and vision of maestro scrum-half Ken Catchpole.

Greg Cornelsen beat a select field for the No. 8 jumper. A superhero of rugby folklore, he remains the only man in history to score four tries against the All Blacks in a Test match. A superb physical specimen, he edged Mark Loane and Toutai Kefu because of his superior lineout ability. George Smith was a freak and staked an irresistible claim at openside flanker. Simon Poidevin brings aggression and bravery on the blindside and complements a well-balanced back row. 'Mr Perfect' John Eales is joined by fellow Queensland hard man Graham Cooke whose Wallaby career spanned 16 seasons either side of the Second World War. In the front row, hooker Phil Kearns pips Peter Johnson and Tommy Lawton. Three World Cups (and two wins) is hard to ignore. William 'Wild Bill' Cerutti nails down tight-head prop to anchor the scrum ahead of John Thornett and Ewen McKenzie, and also provides raw aggression and physicality. At loose-head Jon White was a superb technician, a clever reader of the play and a handy jumper at the front of the lineout. Other Immortals to miss the starting lineup are Lynagh, Larkham, Nick Farr-Jones, George Gregan and Trevor Allan. In all cases another Immortal was selected in their position. Scrum-half provided an embarrassment of riches showcasing the immense talent of Catchpole, Farr-Jones, Gregan and Honourable Mention John Hipwell.

There are four Immortals on the bench. In the front row, Thornett, Johnson and Nick Shehadie provide power, skill and vast experience. When Johnson played his last and 42nd Test against France in 1971, he became Australia's most capped player after 13 seasons of distinguished service. Rob Heming

provides cover for second row. An extraordinary jumper, his fitness, mobility and bravery are well documented. The explosive ball carrying and physicality in attack and defence of No. 8 Mark Loane provides massive impact in the back row. He also played a lot of top-level rugby in South Africa at flanker.

The backline bench oozes five-star quality. Farr-Jones edges superstars Gregan and Hipwell. Lynagh was extremely unlucky to miss the starting lineup and gets the nod over brilliant playmaker Larkham. He covers fly-half, centre and even fullback where he played a Test, not to mention his stupendous goalkicking record. Michael was the world's highest point scorer on 911 when he retired. The great Trevor Allan shapes as a super sub with his searing pace and all-action approach.

GORDON'S ALL-TIME WALLABY TEAM

15. Matthew Burke (NSW)

14. Joe Roff (ACT)

13. Cyril Towers (NSW)

12. Tim Horan (QLD)

11. David Campese (NSW)

10. Mark Ella (NSW)

9. Ken Catchpole (NSW)

8. Greg Cornelsen (QLD)

7. George Smith (ACT)

6. Simon Poidevin (NSW)

5. John Eales (QLD)

4. Graham Cooke (QLD)

3. William 'Wild Bill' Cerutti (NSW)

2. Phil Kearns (NSW)

1. Jon White (NSW)

16. Peter Johnson (NSW)

17. John Thornett (NSW)

18. Nick Shehadie (NSW)

19. Rob Heming (NSW)

20. Mark Loane (QLD)

21. Nick Farr-Jones (NSW)

22. Michael Lynagh (QLD)

23. Trevor Allan (NSW)

ACKNOWLEDGEMENTS

Special thanks go to Luke West at Rockpool Publishing who initially approached me about taking on the *Immortals of Australian Rugby Union*. His positive support and helpful advice throughout the project ensured a smooth passage. Luke allowed me a free hand to make my selections and that level of trust was greatly appreciated.

The team at Rockpool Publishing/Gelding Street Press, led by Lisa Hanrahan and Paul Dennett, also warrant special gratitude for having faith in my knowledge and ability to successfully deliver a worthwhile outcome. I dare to hope that editor Heather Millar found my style manageable and I sincerely thank her for the skilful finishing touches she applied.

Former head of ABC-TV Sport, David Salter, was my writing consultant and backup editorial prompter. An alumnus of my old school, Homebush Boys' High, he was a gifted student with a love of sport and a sharp academic bent (in stark contrast to my blinkered but passionate focus on all things rugby and cricket). Thank you David for your highly valued support.

Distinguished Wallaby Dick Marks was the inaugural national coaching director for 21 years and is a truly iconic figure in Australian rugby history. He provided many positive and insightful opinions on a host of Wallaby legends. As a player he was at the heart of the great revival of Australian rugby in the 1960s. Dick then became director of the newly established National Coaching Panel that eventually led Australia to the summit of world rugby. He has been a friend and confidant to all of our most successful Wallaby coaches. What a treat it was having his input.

Thanks also to my trusted and respected sources, all with long and passionate involvement in the game. I deeply appreciated their objective offerings. And finally, where would I be without my wife Catherine? My greatest and most loyal supporter keeps me on track, tolerates my idiosyncratic ways and is always by my side.

BIBLIOGRAPHY

In many ways this book is a compilation of a lifelong exposure to rugby union. My arrival into this world in 1949 coincided with the historic feat by Trevor Allan's Wallabies who won the Bledisloe Cup in New Zealand after a 15-year hiatus. Nearly 31 years later, that same Wallaby skipper was my designated expert at the SCG for my television Test commentary debut, also against the All Blacks. I have enjoyed professional and social contact with all of the Immortals and Honourable Mentions in this book and conducted multiple interviews with most. That vast reservoir of knowledge, perception and appreciation has been gathered via countless rugby commentary assignments around the globe over the past 50 years. My extensive rugby library and scrapbook collection has also helped facilitate this exciting journey of investigation, assessment and ultimate recognition of our greatest Wallabies. The listing below encompasses the many sources used for content, context, quotes and statistics.

BOOKS

Batchelor, Denzil, *Days Without Sunset*, Eyre & Spottiswoode, London, 1949.

Blucher, Michael, *PERFECT UNION – The parallel lives of Wallaby centres TIM HORAN and JASON LITTLE*, Pan Macmillan Australia Pty Ltd, Sydney, 1995.

Bray, Gordon, *The Australian Rugby Companion – The Game They Play In Heaven*, Penguin Books Australia Ltd, Camberwell, Victoria, 2003.

Bray, Gordon, *From The Ruck*, Random House Australia Pty Ltd, Sydney, 1997.

Chester, RH and McMillan NAC, *The Visitors*, Moa Publications, Auckland, 1990.

Chester, RH and McMillan NAC, *New Zealand Rugby Almanack* (various editions), Moa Publications.

Clark, David, *David CAMPESE*, Pan Macmillan Australia Pty Ltd/ Ironbark, Sydney, 1996.

Curran, James, *CAMPESE – The Last of the Dream Sellers*, Scribe Publications, Melbourne, 2021.

Edwards, Gareth, *100 Great Rugby Players*, Queen Anne Press, London, 1987.

Fenton, Peter, *The Last of His Tribe – ERIC TWEEDALE,* The Rugby Press, Sydney, 2021.

Fenton, Peter, *For The Sake of the Game – 1927/28 Waratahs,* Little Hills Press Pty Ltd, Sydney, 1996.

FitzSimons, Peter, *Nick FARR-JONES – The Authorised Biography,* Random House Australia Pty Ltd, Sydney, 1993.

FitzSimons Peter, *JOHN EALES – The Biography,* ABC Books, Sydney, 2001.

Guinness, Rupert, *George SMITH,* Allen & Unwin, Sydney, 2011.

Harris, Brett & Ella, Mark, *ELLA – The Definitive Biography,* Random House Australia Pty Ltd, Sydney, 2007.

Hauser, Liam, *Immortals of Australian Rugby League,* Rockpool Publishing, Sydney, 2019.

Heads, Ian, *Matthew BURKE – A rugby life,* Pan Macmillan Australia Pty Ltd, Sydney, 2005.

Howell, Max, *Born to Lead,* Celebrity Books, Auckland, 2005.

Howell, Max and Xie, Lingyu, *Wallaby Greats,* Rugby Publishing Ltd, Auckland 1996.

Howell, Max and Xie, Lingyu, Wilkes, Bensley, *THE WALLABIES – A Definitive History of Australian Test Rugby,* GAP Publishing, Norman Park, Queensland, 2000.

Howell, Max and Xie, Lingyu, Neazor, Paul, Wilkes, Bensley, *THEY CAME TO CONQUER – VOLUMES I AND II,* Howell-Xie Publishing Company Pty Ltd, Brisbane, 2003.

Howitt, Bob, *DB Rugby Annual,* Moa Publications, Auckland, 1978.

Howitt, Bob, *DB Rugby Annual,* Moa Publications, Auckland, 1982.

Jenkins, Peter, *Wallaby Gold – The History of Australian Test Rugby,* Random House Australia, Sydney, 2003.

Jenkinson, Mike, *A Dangerous Breed,* Jenkinson Consulting Pty Ltd, Hobart 2018.

Laidlaw, Chris, *Mud in Your Eye,* A.H. & A.W. Reed Ltd, Wellington, 1973.

Larkham, Stephen, *Stephen Larkham's WORLD CUP DIARY,* Penguin Books Australia, Camberwell, Victoria, 2004.

McRae, Donald, *EDDIE JONES – My Life and Rugby: The Autobiography,* Macmillan, London, 2019.

Meares, Peter & Max Howell, *WALLABY Legends,* Thomas C. Lothian Pty Ltd, Melbourne, 2005.

McGee, Greg, *Richie McCAW – The Open Side,* Hachette New Zealand Ltd/A Hodder Moa book, Auckland, 2012.

Parker, A.C., *The Springboks,* Cassell & Company Ltd, Johannesburg, 1970.

Pollard, Jack, *Australian Rugby – The Game and the Players,* Pan Macmillan Australia Pty Ltd / Ironbark, Sydney, 1994.

Robertson, Ian, *The Complete Book of the Rugby World Cup 1999*, Hodder and Stoughton, London, 1999.

Sharpham, Peter, *The First Wallabies,* Sandstone Publishing, Sydney, 2000.

Shehadie, Sir Nicholas, *A Life Worth Living,* Simon & Schuster (Australia) Pty Ltd, Sydney, 2003.

Slack, Andrew, *NODDY – The Authorised Biography of Michael Lynagh,* William Heinemann Australia a part of Reed Books Australia, Melbourne, 1995.

Verdon, Paul, *LEGENDS of World Rugby,* Hill-Verdon Publishing Ltd, Auckland, 2007.

Webster, Jim, *POIDEVIN – For Love Not Money,* ABC Enterprises, Sydney, 1992.

West, Luke, *Immortals of Australian Motor Racing – The Local Heroes,* Rockpool Publishing, Sydney, 2021.

Zavos, Spiro and Bray, Gordon, *Two Mighty Tribes, The Story of the All Blacks vs the Wallabies*: Penguin Books Australia, Camberwell, Victoria, 2003.

Zavos, Spiro, *The Golden Wallabies – The Story of Australia's Rugby World Champions,* Penguin Books Australia Ltd, Ringwood, Victoria, 2000.

NEWSPAPERS

Daily Express (UK)
Daily Mail (UK)
The Argus (South Africa)
The Australian
The Courier Mail
The Daily Telegraph
The Gympie Times
The Sydney Morning Herald

WEBSITES

rugby.com.au
espnscrum.com

VIDEO

Theo Clark, *Sometimes the Best Ever,* Theo Clark Media, Sydney.

Theo Clark, *Remembering Norths: The 1960s Golden Era,* Theo Clark Media, Sydney.

ABOUT THE AUTHOR

Gordon Bray was renowned throughout Australia for more than four decades as the 'Voice of Rugby'. He is one of our longest serving sports commentators having started with the ABC in 1969 as a specialist trainee. His name is synonymous with televised rugby union and his distinctive commentary style remains as much a part of the Australian game as a George Gregan tackle or a David Campese goose-step.

As a schoolboy scrum-half, Bray captained the First XV at Homebush Boys High to a premiership before joining Eastern Suburbs DRUFC. Later, as an accomplished referee, he was appointed to 199 games by the NSW Rugby Referees Association. Gordon called his first rugby Test match on radio for the ABC in Bordeaux in 1976 and is still adamant Australia was robbed of a famous victory over France that day by a tardy Scottish referee who found himself 'a mile behind the play'. Since then Bray has called more than 350 Test matches. In 1980 he succeeded the legendary Norman May as the ABC's rugby union commentator on television and called every milestone victory by the Wallabies over the next 40 years, including both Rugby World Cup triumphs. He was also at Brighton, England, behind the ITV microphone in 2015 when minnow Japan downed two-time World Cup champions South Africa in one of the biggest boilovers in sporting history.

After 25 years with ABC Sport he moved to commercial television and spent 16 years at the Seven Network and 10 years at Ten. Renowned for his versatility, Gordon has called over 25 sports at international level and covered 10 Olympic Games after making his Commonwealth Games debut at Christchurch in 1974 and Olympic debut two years later in Montreal. Bray is the author and editor of seven books on rugby union including bestsellers *From the Ruck* and *The Australian Rugby Companion*. He was made a Member of the Order of Australia in 2005, is a past recipient of the prestigious Penguin Award for sports broadcasting, an inductee into the SCG Media Hall of Honour and is an ambassador for Legacy Australia. Prolific author and newspaper columnist Peter FitzSimons has described Bray as 'more than a sporting icon, Gordon is no less than the soundtrack of our sporting lives'.

ALSO IN THE SERIES

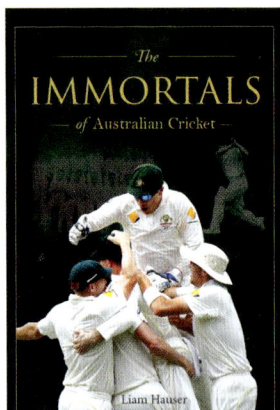

The Immortals of Australian Cricket
by Liam Hauser
ISBN: 9781925682786

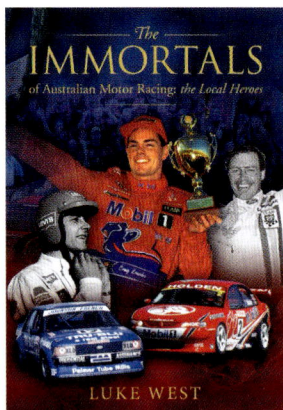

The Immortals of Australian Motor Racing: the Local Heroes
by Luke West
ISBN: 9781925946987

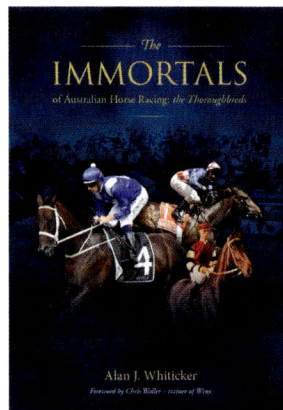

The Immortals of Australian Horse Racing: the Thoroughbreds
by Alan J. Whiticker
ISBN: 9781925946963

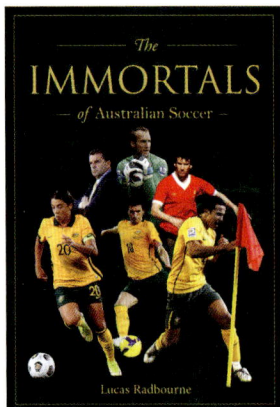

The Immortals of Australian Soccer
by Lucas Radbourne
ISBN: 9781922579355

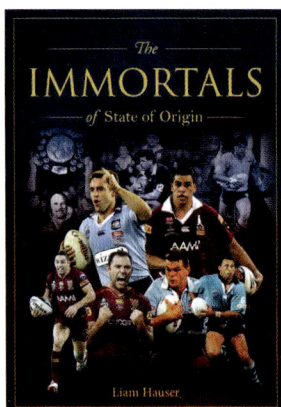

The Immortals of State of Origin
by Liam Hauser
ISBN: 9781922579799

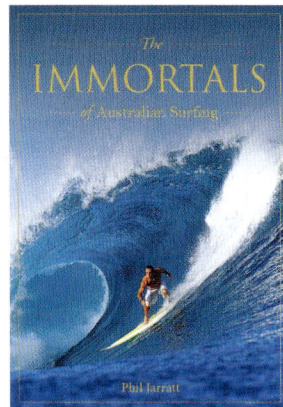

The Immortals of Australian Surfing
by Phil Jarratt
ISBN: 9780645207095

Available now from all good book stores.
www.geldingstreetpress.com

CYRIL TOWERS · TREVOR ALLAN · JOH
OIDEVIN · MARK ELLA · DAVID CAMPE
M HORAN · JOHN EALES · MATTHEW
ARKHAM · GEORGE SMITH · CYRIL TO
EN CATCHPOLE · SIMON POIDEVIN ·
YNAGH · NICK FARR-JONES · TIM HO
EORGE GREGAN · STEPHEN LARKHAM
LLAN · JOHN THORNETT · KEN CATC
AMPESE · MICHAEL LYNAGH · NICK F
ATTHEW BURKE · GEORGE GREGAN ·
OWERS · TREVOR ALLAN · JOHN THO
ARK ELLA · DAVID CAMPESE · MICHA
OHN EALES · MATTHEW BURKE · GEO
MITH · CYRIL TOWERS · TREVOR ALL
MON POIDEVIN · MARK ELLA · DAVI
ONES · TIM HORAN · JOHN EALES · M
ARKHAM · GEORGE SMITH · CYRIL TO
EN CATCHPOLE · SIMON POIDEVIN ·
YNAGH · NICK FARR-JONES · TIM HO
EORGE GREGAN · STEPHEN LARKHAM
LLAN · JOHN THORNETT · KEN CATC
AMPESE · MICHAEL LYNAGH · NICK

CYRIL TOWERS · TREVOR ALLAN · JOH
OIDEVIN · MARK ELLA · DAVID CAMP
M HORAN · JOHN EALES · MATTHEW
ARKHAM · GEORGE SMITH · CYRIL TO
EN CATCHPOLE · SIMON POIDEVIN
NAGH · NICK FARR-JONES · TIM HO
EORGE GREGAN · STEPHEN LARKHAM
LLAN · JOHN THORNETT · KEN CATC
AMPESE · MICHAEL LYNAGH · NICK
ATTHEW BURKE · GEORGE GREGAN ·
OWERS · TREVOR ALLAN · JOHN THO
ARK ELLA · DAVID CAMPESE · MICHA
OHN EALES · MATTHEW BURKE · GEO
MITH · CYRIL TOWERS · TREVOR ALL
MON POIDEVIN · MARK ELLA · DAVI
ONES · TIM HORAN · JOHN EALES · M
ARKHAM · GEORGE SMITH · CYRIL TO
EN CATCHPOLE · SIMON POIDEVIN
NAGH · NICK FARR-JONES · TIM HO
EORGE GREGAN · STEPHEN LARKHAM
LLAN · JOHN THORNETT · KEN CATC
AMPESE · MICHAEL LYNAGH · NICK